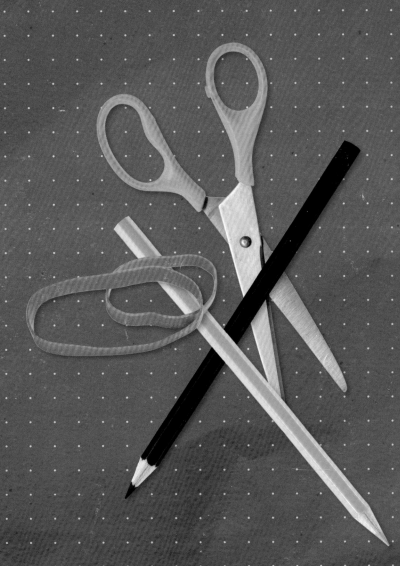

BALLOON CAR

NATIONAL
GEOGRAPHIC
KiDS

MAKE THIS!

BUILDING, THINKING, AND TINKERING PROJECTS FOR THE AMAZING MAKER IN YOU

ELLA SCHWARTZ

PHOTOGRAPHS BY
MATTHEW RAKOLA

NATIONAL GEOGRAPHIC
WASHINGTON, D.C.

TABLE OF CONTENTS

BELT MOVER

CHAPTER 1

RESCUE A DINOSAUR

CHAPTER 2

CHAPTER 3

COLOR
KALEIDOSCOPE

FOREWORD

MAKING IS A PART OF HUMAN NATURE. IT IS ONE OF THE MAIN WAYS THAT WE INTERACT WITH THE WORLD AROUND US.

Nearly everything we touch on a daily basis was dreamed up, invented, used, or made by another person. It is through making that we can shape, understand, and control the world around us. Whether it is as simple as crafting a meal from basic food ingredients or as complicated as developing a new type of computer, making allows us to simplify our daily lives and also to solve some of the biggest problems this planet has ever faced.

If you look back through history, some of the greatest minds were makers. These innovators dreamed up new ideas that would fundamentally change the world they lived in—and the world we live in today. Leonardo da Vinci, the famous Renaissance man, was an inventor of flying machines that wouldn't come to life until hundreds of years later. Alexander Graham Bell, one of the founders of the National Geographic Society, invented the telephone, which paved the way for modern communication, television, and the internet. Ada Lovelace, the first computer programmer, made humanity's first attempt at writing software on early mechanical computers. Hedy Lamarr, a famous actress from the 1940s, invented and patented technology that ultimately brought us Wi-Fi, GPS, and Bluetooth. Even ice cream was made possible through a small machine invented by maker Nancy Johnson in the mid-1800s. In fact, humans have made so much that there are now more transistors, the building blocks of modern electronics, on Earth than leaves on all the trees in every forest on this planet.

Makers build the world around us. They create the cities that we live in and the items that influence how we live our daily lives. From traffic lights to toaster ovens, every single human-made item you use each day is the result of a creative maker tinkering around

in an attempt to solve a problem. Every invention starts as an idea in someone's head, becomes an experiment, and then gets made real in the hands of a maker. Oftentimes, those ideas take years to develop. But through experimentation, creating prototypes, and testing how and why the prototypes fail, makers follow their curiosity through the whole development process until they finally come to solutions that work.

For me, I have always known that I wanted to be a maker. I was that curious kid who would find a screwdriver and take apart anything I could get my hands on ... including things like my dad's expensive music equipment. But instead of getting upset, my dad would just teach me how to put it all back together again. My love for making came from learning about how things worked during those days with my dad. And that led me to study engineering in college. In my first job as a professional engineer, I worked on making rocket engines for spacecraft. Yes, I'm a real-life rocket scientist! During that time, my team launched 13 satellites into orbit around Earth. You may have even used some of my satellites to communicate with friends, watch television, or listen to the radio.

I loved being a rocket scientist, but I wanted to do so much more for the world. I wanted to use my maker skills to solve big problems. So I became a conservation technologist. That's an engineer who builds technology to help better protect, understand, and monitor wildlife. I've built tools that help us map gorilla habitats in Congo, observe elephants in protected reserves, track sperm whales in Antarctica, and monitor fish and water quality throughout the Amazon rain forest. For all of these projects, I used skills similar to the ones you'll use in this book. Today, I even have my own makerspace dedicated entirely to conservation technology. There, we dream up ideas, prototype, build, and test them. Sometimes our experiments fail, but we just use that as a learning experience to make it better the next time. Dreaming, testing, failing, and revising are all part of making!

Making is easier than it has ever been before. The internet has made access to information, parts, help, and projects just a click away. You can even be an inventor without leaving your couch! You can design a part, send it to a 3D-printing center, have it built, tested, and mailed to your front door—all with a few clicks on a computer. But no matter how easy it may be to get the parts you need, it's the creative, problem-solving, try-and-try-again attitude that drives making.

As you look through this book and try some of these challenges, think about problems around you that can be solved by some of these tools and techniques. You will be surprised at how often a maker skill can help you in different parts of your life! Don't be afraid to have some big ideas as well. We need your help to make a better future for every person, animal, and robot on this planet! Maybe one of you will become a conservation technologist, too, and help us protect lions, hippos, wolves, sharks, and all the other amazing animals that roam free in the wild.

Makers shape the world around them, and I can't wait to see what you'll come up with. Don't give up on your dreams and never stop exploring!

—SHAH SELBE
National Geographic Fellow and Conservation Technologist

This is my conservation technology makerspace, where we build all the technology we take on expeditions.

WHAT IS A MAKER?

A MAKER IS SOMEONE WHO TINKERS, FIXES, BREAKS, REBUILDS, AND CONSTRUCTS PROJECTS FOR THE WORLD AROUND THEM.

When faced with a problem, a maker can use or recycle materials around them to solve it. A maker may not solve the problem on the first try, but that's not a big deal. Makers aren't afraid to fail. It's just another chance to try again and again to come up with the perfect solution—maybe! It's part of the challenge and the fun!

There is no one kind of maker. Makers are artists, crafters, bakers, builders, painters, woodworkers, inventors, and more. A maker is anyone who is curious and creative.

A MAKER IS YOU!

MAKER-SPACES

SO, LET'S GET STARTED. FIRST, YOU'RE GOING TO NEED A MAKERSPACE. A MAKERSPACE IS AN AREA WHERE MAKERS WORK.

A makerspace doesn't have to be anything fancy. It's just a designated place where you're free to create and explore. Your makerspace might be in your house, school, or library. Some makerspaces might be rooms filled with high-tech tools and gadgets. These makerspaces may have equipment like 3D printers, computers, sewing machines, power tools, and construction materials. Other makerspaces are simpler. They may include nothing more than a small desk with craft supplies. As long as you have a place to work, some basic supplies, and your imagination, you're in business!

MAKER-BOXES

SOMETHING USEFUL FOR A MAKER TO HAVE IN THEIR MAKERSPACE IS A MAKERBOX.

A makerbox is a place to keep all your essential maker tools. Everyone's makerbox is different depending on interests, but here are a few ideas to get you started!

MAKERS REUSE!

Sometimes gadgets or toys around the house break. Whenever something breaks, it's always a good idea to ask an adult if it's possible to fix it before throwing it away. But if it can't be fixed, you may be able to reuse parts from the item. Add it to your makerbox.

MAKERS RECYCLE!

You can find awesome maker supplies from scraps around your house. A few suggestions are:

- Cereal boxes
- Plastic bottles
- Empty, clean food containers
- Egg cartons
- Empty spools of thread
- Empty toilet paper or paper towel tubes
- Bottle caps
- Scraps of paper
- Wooden chopsticks

MAKERS CREATE!

Your makerbox should be a handy place to include all the tools you may need to design and build your creations. Some items you probably want to include in your makerbox are:

- Paper and pencils for drafting designs and recording results
- Rubber bands
- Tape
- Glue
- Paper clips
- String
- Craft sticks

Most importantly, a makerbox is a work in progress. Over time, makers will add items to grow and improve their makerbox. There's no need to have the perfect makerbox to get started. Have fun adding materials to your makerbox as you continue to explore and grow as a maker.

READY TO TRY TINKERING LIKE A MAKER? Here we go!

DISSECT A TOY CHALLENGE

Have you ever wondered what's inside your old toys? In this activity, you'll find out.

STEP 1

SELECT A NON-ELECTRICAL TOY.

You'll be taking the toy apart, so be sure to pick one that no one in your family wants anymore. (It's a good idea to ask permission from everyone in your family!) Consider toys that:

- are old or broken already
- roll, dance, or move without batteries or electronics
- produce sounds (like a harmonica or kazoo)

This activity also works well with other objects you may find around your house.

STEP 2

PLAN YOUR DISSECTION.

Now that you've selected a toy, it's time to plan how to go about the dissection. First, take a close look at how your toy is built. Start by looking at the individual parts of your toy.

- How many individual parts does the toy have?
- Do you see how the parts come together? Are screws used to fasten the parts together? Is there a seam where fabric comes together to join the parts? Are the parts glued together?
- What do you think is the purpose of each individual part? Can you guess how the parts come together on the inside to make the toy work?

Now that you've looked carefully at the parts, think about the best way to dissect the toy. You'll need to select the right tools to get the job done. Is the toy fastened together with screws? If yes, you'll probably need a screwdriver. Does it contain fabric? Perhaps a pair of scissors would help get inside. Can you think of other tools that might be helpful for this job?

WARNING Some toys or household items should not be used for this activity. Anything that plugs into a wall or uses a battery is not a good choice. Toys that contain glass or liquid should also be avoided. Ask a grown-up to help you decide whether something is safe to take apart so you can proceed with caution.

STEP 3

START DISSECTING.

You're ready to get inside your toy. Use the tools you've selected to start taking it apart. Remove one part at a time. Work carefully and slowly, paying special attention to how everything is connected. For example, if you see a gear, you may not want to remove it too quickly. You may want to first trace along the gear's path to see what it is connected to. This might give you a clue about what it controls and how the toy operates.

As you work, explore the toy's insides. Try to guess what each of the parts might be used for. If your toy was broken, can you figure out why it was broken? Perhaps a piece is loose or a connecting piece has been dislodged?

Take notes on what you see. Draw sketches of the toy's insides and all its visible parts. Write down your impressions on what you think each part is for. Continue to document what you see as you work and observe.

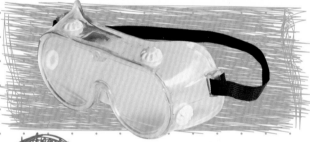

Always use appropriate safety equipment. Safety glasses are recommended.

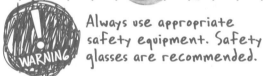

It's a good idea to have a pencil and paper handy. Jot down your predictions before you get started. What do you think you'll see once you get inside the toy?

STEP 4

KEEP GOING!

You've taken apart your toy, but is there a piece that can be broken down even more? Try to take your toy down to its smallest pieces. Don't forget to take step-by-step notes as you work to help you remember the original configuration of your toy.

STEP 5

NOW WHAT?

So you've dissected a toy. Congratulations! Now what are you going to do?

- Now that you've taken your toy apart, can you put it back together again? Use the notes you took during the dissection to help you. If you had to break something to get inside, it may not be possible to put it back together to its original form. That's okay!
- Make a new contraption from the dissected toy parts. You can even dissect more than one toy and combine parts and pieces from several toys to make a crazy new toy.
- Can you salvage any parts from your toy to reuse or recycle? It's a good idea to add these parts to your makerbox for future maker projects.

So how is taking something apart *making*, you ask? Well, knowing how something comes apart can tell you a lot about how it comes together! The more you know about how things work, the more solutions might come to mind when faced with a challenge. And that's important for makers.

This knowledge can help makers find solutions to challenges in the world around them. The more makers tinker, assemble, create, reuse, and recycle, the more problems they can solve.

THINK YOU'RE UP TO THE CHALLENGE? Let's go!

HOW TO USE THIS BOOK

Some of the activities in this book include step-by-step instructions to help you become a pro maker. Other activities are open-ended, with no right or wrong approach. These challenges will test your imagination to solve a problem.

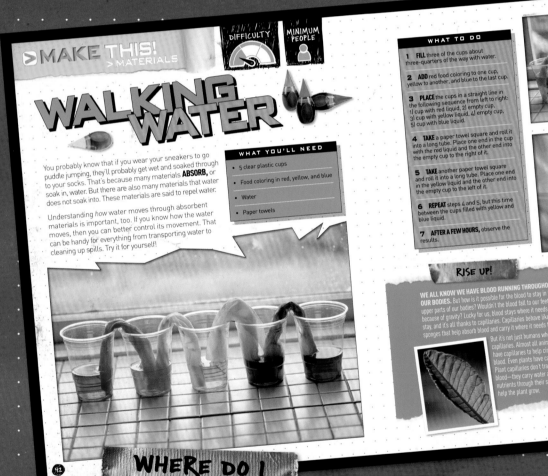

>MAKE THIS!
>MATERIALS

DIFFICULTY

MINIMUM PEOPLE

WALKING WATER

You probably know that if you wear your sneakers to go puddle jumping, they'll probably get wet and soaked through to your socks. That's because many materials **ABSORB**, or soak in, water. But there are also many materials that water does not soak into. These materials are said to repel water.

Understanding how water moves through absorbent materials is important, too. If you know how the water moves, then you can better control its movement. That can be handy for everything from transporting water to cleaning up spills. Try it for yourself!

WHAT YOU'LL NEED

- 5 clear plastic cups
- Food coloring in red, yellow, and blue
- Water
- Paper towels

WHAT TO DO

1 **FILL** three of the cups about three-quarters of the way with water.

2 **ADD** red food coloring to one cup, yellow to another, and blue to the last cup.

3 **PLACE** the cups in a straight line in the following sequence from left to right: 1) cup with red liquid, 2) empty cup, 3) cup with yellow liquid, 4) empty cup, 5) cup with blue liquid.

4 **TAKE** a paper towel square and roll it into a long tube. Place one end in the cup with the red liquid and the other end into the empty cup to the right of it.

5 **TAKE** another paper towel square and roll it into a long tube. Place one end in the yellow liquid and the other end into the empty cup to the left of it.

6 **REPEAT** steps 4 and 5, but this time between the cups filled with yellow and blue liquid.

7 **AFTER A FEW HOURS,** observe the results.

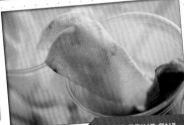

WHAT'S GOING ON?

Paper towels are made of a material that is highly absorbent. The water is soaked up by the paper towel and moved into the empty cups. The process where liquid moves up something solid, like a paper towel, is known as capillary action. Capillary action is what makes water move or "walk" up the paper towels and into the empty cup. The empty cup fills up with water until the water levels of all the cups are equal. When red mixes with yellow it makes the color orange. When yellow mixes with blue it makes the color green.

THINK ABOUT IT

What if you tried this experiment with other materials, like old socks, instead of paper towels? What if instead of water you used other liquids, like vinegar or oil? Do you think you would get similar results?

RISE UP!

WE ALL KNOW WE HAVE BLOOD RUNNING THROUGHOUT OUR BODIES. But how is it possible for the blood to stay in the upper parts of our bodies? Wouldn't the blood fall to our feet because of gravity? Lucky for us, blood stays where it needs to stay, and its all thanks to capillaries. Capillaries behave like little sponges that help absorb blood and carry it where it needs to go.

But it's not just humans who have capillaries. Almost all animals have capillaries to help circulate blood. Even plants have capillaries. Plant capillaries don't transport blood—they carry water and nutrients through their stems to help the plant grow.

42

WHERE DO I START?

Anywhere you want!

IF YOU'RE LOOKING FOR SOME STEP-BY-STEP INSTRUCTIONS TO MAKE AWESOME CREATIONS— from Skee-Ball games to fidget spinners—the Make This! activities are the place for you.

SOLVE THIS!
> MATERIALS

The materials you choose can have lots of effects on the final product. Take a look at these scenarios, then grab your makerbox. Can you tinker up some solutions using the best materials? Remember, there's no right answer!

IF YOU WANT TO STRETCH YOUR CEREBRUM, check out the Solve This! challenges. Each super scenario puts your problem-solving smarts to the test. Grab your makerbox and start tinkering! You never know what awesome solutions you'll devise.

SITUATION #1

You're a biologist tracking a family of mountain gorillas in central Africa.

So far, everything's going great. There's just one problem. Mosquitoes bother you all day and now you're itchy all the time. How can you protect yourself from mosquitoes without disturbing the gorillas while you observe them?

SITUATION #3

You're a botanist trying to understand why a farm's crops are not thriving, even though the farmers insist they are watering the fields every day.

You take a look at the soil the crops are planted in. It's dry, and the soil particles are large. Soil that contains larger particles has a hard time absorbing water because water passes too quickly through the larger gaps. How can you improve the flow of water to the crops?

SITUATION #4

You're a scientist working in the Amazon rain forest studying the interaction between plants, animals, and the environment.

Your field work requires a lot of equipment to help you collect samples and measure data. There's one big problem: The lab equipment isn't waterproof, and here in the rain forest, frequent rainstorms are a good bet. What kind of canopy can you devise to help keep your equipment dry while diverting rainwater away from your work area?

SOME HELPFUL HINTS TO GET YOU STARTED

- **EACH MAKE THIS! ACTIVITY INCLUDES A LIST OF MATERIALS COMMONLY FOUND AT HOME.** Don't have something on the list? Get creative! The best part of making is improvising. What other materials could you swap in for the stuff you don't have? What materials behave the same way or would get you to the same result? Try a few and find out!

- **NOT SURE WHERE TO START WITH A SOLVE THIS! SCENARIO?** Take a look at the Make This! activities that come before it. Chances are you'll find some inspiration (and some super-helpful science and engineering info) to get your mind whirring.

- **IS ONE OF YOUR SOLUTIONS NOT WORKING? KEEP TINKERING!** Think like an engineer and try to break down where exactly the trouble spot is. Ask yourself questions: At what point does it seem to stop working properly? What materials or factors are involved in that spot? What changes could you make to each material or factor? Try changing just one item at a time. That will help you pinpoint the trouble.

- **REMEMBER: IF YOU HAVE A QUESTION, SOMEONE PROBABLY HAS AN IDEA!** If you're stuck, need inspiration, or just want to gather a few ideas before you get started, ask around! Try your friends, family, teachers, siblings, hamster … they all have different experiences and perspectives. And sometimes, just talking about a question out loud is enough to spark a brainstorm.

CHAPTER 1

SIMPLE MACHINES

QUICK FACTS

WHEN YOU NEED TO MOVE ANYTHING FROM ONE PLACE TO ANOTHER, usually that involves pulling, pushing, or lifting. In science, the energy you use to move something is called **WORK.**

There are TWO FACTORS that affect WORK:

EFFORT

HOW MUCH EFFORT IT TAKES TO MOVE SOMETHING

Moving a pebble from point A to point B takes a lot less work than moving a boulder from point A to point B. The distance may be the same, but because the boulder is a lot heavier than the pebble, moving it takes more effort, which means more work.

DISTANCE

THE DISTANCE THE THING IS MOVED

Imagine you're holding a brick above the ground, with your arm out straight in front of you. It takes a lot of effort to keep holding the heavy brick, but you're not actually doing any work, as defined by science. That's because the brick isn't moving. No work is done unless you move the brick. Now, if instead of holding your arm steady you lift the brick, then you'd be performing work.

SIMPLE MACHINES

DEVICES THAT MAKE THE EFFORT OF MOVING SOMETHING EASIER

The work may be the same, but it takes a lot less effort with simple machines. There are six types of simple machines. They have been used for thousands of years as tools to make moving things much easier.

PULLEY

LEVER

WHEEL & AXLE

INCLINED PLANE

WEDGE

SCREW

LET'S EXPLORE WAYS THEY MAKE MOVING THINGS EASIER.

DIFFICULTY

MINIMUM PEOPLE

ROLLING PIN PULLEY

It's not easy lifting heavy objects with muscle power alone.
Need to haul a stack of big books up a staircase? Or how about moving a piano to the top floor of an apartment building? That's where a **PULLEY** can be very handy. Pulleys make the effort of lifting and moving heavy objects much easier. Try it for yourself!

WHAT YOU'LL NEED

- A heavy book

- 8 to 10 feet (2.4 to 3 m) of heavy string or rope

- A rolling pin

- Two friends

WHAT TO DO

1 **LOOP** the string or rope around the book several times, in different directions, and tie it securely in place.

2 **PLACE** the book on the ground. Try lifting the book by slowly pulling up on the loose end of the string. Note how much effort you felt you needed.

3 **ASK** two friends to hold the rolling pin securely, so it doesn't move.

4 **DRAPE** the loose end of the string over the rolling pin.

5 **SLOWLY PULL** down on the string to lift the books.

Was it easier to lift the book by pulling up on the string, or by pulling down on the string over the rolling pin?

WHAT'S GOING ON?

Lifting a heavy object with a string is hard. When you lift the same object by placing the string over a rolling pin it is much easier. That is because it is always easier to pull down than to pull up. Pulling up means you're fighting against gravity. When you pull down, you have gravity helping you, so it requires less effort.

THINK ABOUT IT

Can you think of a way to make lifting the book even easier? What if you had another friend and two rolling pins?

PULLEY SPOTTER

THERE ARE PULLEYS ALL AROUND YOU!
Can you spot them in your own house? Here's a hint: Take a close look at your curtains. What about pulleys at school? Does your school have a flag pole? What mechanism does it use to raise the flag? You guessed it! A pulley. Can you spot pulleys in your neighborhood? Pulleys are everywhere. Try keeping a list and see how many you can spot today.

PENCIL PUSHER

WHEELS help make the work of moving things from one place to another much easier. Imagine trying to push a shopping cart through the grocery store aisles if the cart didn't have any wheels! You might be able to do it, but it would be much harder. An **AXLE** is a rod attached to the middle of two wheels. The axle helps the wheels move together to push along the heavy thing. Try it for yourself!

WHAT YOU'LL NEED

- A heavy book or stack of books

- 8 round pencils

- A long empty table or hardwood floor

WHAT TO DO

1 **GENTLY PUSH** the book all the way across the length of the table or a few feet (about a meter) across the floor.

2 **NOW ARRANGE** the pencils parallel to each other, spaced about an inch (2.5 cm) apart.

3 **LAY** the book across the pencils and gently roll the book forward.

Was it easier to push the book across the table, or to roll the book across the pencils?

WHAT'S GOING ON?

Pushing the heavy book across the table or floor takes a lot of effort. This is because as you push the book, the surface of the table or floor is providing some resistance against the book. This resistance is called friction. To push the book against the surface, you are fighting against the force of friction. It's much easier to roll the book across the surface because you encounter less friction. Since the pencils are round, they allow the heavy book to be rolled along a path—like wheels.

THE MYSTERY OF STONEHENGE

Stonehenge is a stone monument in England that is a big mystery! It was built from extremely heavy slabs of stone, thousands of years ago. Scientists know that the stone had come from the coast of Wales, 160 miles (257 km) away from the Stonehenge site. That means the stone was somehow transported over a great distance without wagons, carts, or any other sophisticated vehicle.

HOW IS THAT POSSIBLE?

The stones were extremely heavy, so lifting the stone would have been next to impossible, even for a team of people.

SO HOW DID THEY DO IT?

Many people believe the builders of Stonehenge used a system similar to the one used in this activity.

23

MAKE THIS!
> SIMPLE MACHINES

DIFFICULTY

MINIMUM PEOPLE

GRAB AN ADULT!

BELT MOVER

We already know that using simple machines makes transporting things much easier. A **CONVEYOR BELT** uses simple machines, like wheels or pulleys, to move things along a continuous belt. As the belt moves forward it moves objects placed on the belt forward with it. Using a conveyor belt makes the job of moving things from one location to another easier and faster. Try it for yourself!

WHAT YOU'LL NEED

- 1 sheet of white printer paper
- Ruler
- Scissors
- 1 cardboard half-gallon milk carton, cleaned and dried
- 2 pencils
- Tape
- A pen or marker for writing

1 **HOLDING THE PAPER** the tall way, measure across with the ruler, with 0 at the left end of the paper. Make a mark with your pen at 2¼ inches (5.7 cm), 5½ inches (14 cm), and 6¾ inches (17.1 cm). Make these same three marks at different spots down the paper. Then use the ruler to draw long straight lines from the top to the bottom of the paper, passing through each mark. Use the scissors to cut along the lines to create three identical strips of paper that are each 2¼ inches (5.7 cm) wide and 11 inches (27.9 cm) long. You can recycle the rest of the paper.

2 **USING THE TAPE,** secure the three strips together so you have one extra-long continuous strip of paper. Be sure to tape the strips together tightly.

3 **CUT OFF** the pointed top of the container.

4 **NEXT, STAND THE CARTON UP** so that the open part is at the top. Choose two facing sides to cut out. Cut off the two opposite faces of the container, leaving about 2 inches (5 cm) on all sides. Now your container should have two sides and a bottom.

5 **POKE** the pencil through one uncut side of the container, about 4 inches (10 cm) from the bottom, and out through the other side of the container.

6 **POKE** the second pencil through the side of the container, about 4 inches (10 cm) from where the top was, and out through the other side of the container.

7 **TAPE** one end of your extra-long paper securely to the center of one pencil. Roll the pencil so the paper spools around the pencil and until approximately 12 inches (30 cm) of paper remains. Tape the other end of the paper securely to the center of the second pencil. Begin to spool it around the second pencil and continue until the paper is tight.

8 **PLACE** light toys on one end of your conveyor belt. Now spin the two pencils in the same direction. Watch your objects travel down the conveyor belt.

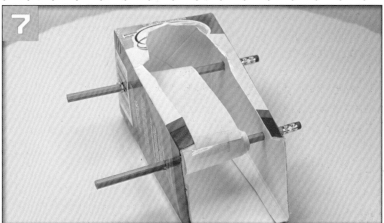

PEOPLE MOVER

AN ESCALATOR MIGHT LOOK LIKE A MOVING STAIRCASE, but it's actually a kind of conveyor belt used to carry people up and down. The stairs are pulled around in a continuous loop, but instead of being horizontal, the loop is sloped.

WHAT'S GOING ON?

The conveyor belt you built uses a continuous strip of paper that rotates around two pencils, which act as axles. As you power the axles in the same direction, the paper belt moves forward, taking the materials on the belt forward with it.

THINK ABOUT IT

What happens when your conveyor belt paper has been completely spooled around the far pencil? Can you reverse the conveyor belt?

SKEE-BALL CHALLENGE

INCLINED PLANES are simple machines with no moving parts. They make it easier for us to move objects to higher surfaces than if we lifted the objects directly upward. But there are trade-offs. A gentle slope requires little effort, but the person must push the object over a longer distance. A steep slope reduces the distance a person must push the object, but increases the effort needed. Try it for yourself!

WHAT YOU'LL NEED

- 2 laundry baskets (medium-size cardboard boxes would work, too)

- 1 large rectangular cardboard box

- Masking tape

- Scissors

- Several plastic balls

- 2 sheets of paper: one labeled 50 points, the other labeled 100 points

WHAT TO DO

1 USING THE SCISSORS, carefully remove, as one piece, the top of the box along with one short side of the box. You will be left with a box that has three sides and a bottom and one long piece of cardboard with a bend.

2 USE the piece you just removed from the box to build a Skee-Ball-style ramp. Tape one short side to the back of the box. Put the other short flat side on the bottom of the box to create a ramp. Experiment with different ramp angles by sliding the short side along the box's bottom. Once you have an angle that you think might work, secure the ramp to the box with the masking tape.

3 TAPE one paper to each of the laundry baskets. These are the targets.

4 PLACE the laundry basket labeled 50 points directly in front of the laundry basket labeled 100 points. Set up the ramp in front of the baskets.

5 TEST your ramp by rolling a ball up the ramp while aiming for one of the point targets. You may need to adjust the position of the ramp or laundry baskets. Experiment by rolling the balls with different amounts of force.

6 GRAB a few friends and play!

💡 THINK ABOUT IT

How would changing the angle of the ramp affect how hard you will need to roll the ball?

WHAT'S GOING ON?

The ramp you built is an inclined plane. Depending on the angle of your ramp, the ball needs a certain amount of force to be rolled all the way up the ramp and into the targets. The steeper the ramp the more force is needed to get the ball up the ramp. This means you're going to need to roll your ball harder. If your ramp is less steep, you may not need to roll the ball with as much force, but the ball would need to travel a longer distance to reach the targets.

DIFFICULTY

MINIMUM PEOPLE

GRAB AN ADULT!

ARCHIMEDES' SCREW

We use **SCREWS** all the time to hold things together. You screw on the cap to a tube of toothpaste or a bottle of juice so the containers are nicely closed. You might use screws to fasten pieces of metal or wood together. But screws can also be used to raise and lower things. In fact, a screw is actually an inclined plane wrapped around a cylinder.

The Archimedes' screw is a simple machine used for transferring water from lower elevations to higher elevations. The ancient Greek mathematician Archimedes is believed to have invented the machine.

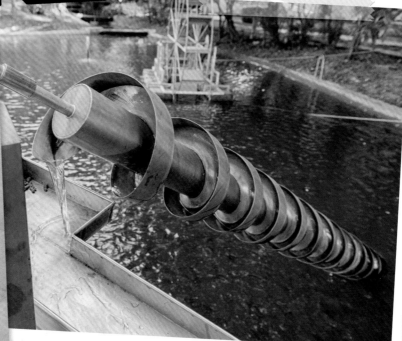

This Archimedes' screw is used to transport water from lower elevations to higher elevations.

FUN FACTS ABOUT SCREWS

- **AS HERMIT CRABS GROW,** their abdomens grow into a "corkscrew" spiral shape that helps them "screw" securely into the shell they choose to live in.
- **SCREWS WERE FIRST USED IN OLIVE PRESSES AND GRAPE PRESSES.** Later, in the Middle Ages, this mechanism was adapted for use in the printing press and the paper press.
- **TODAY SCREWS ARE COMMONLY USED AS FASTENERS,** but screws weren't used as fasteners until the Middle Ages. Some of the earliest screws to be used as fasteners were for military weapons.

WHAT YOU'LL NEED

- A medium-size bowl

- A tall drinking cup

- A piece of PVC pipe 1½ inches (3.8 cm) in diameter and approximately 14 inches (35 cm) long

- Clear plastic tubing, ¼ inch (0.6 cm) inside diameter

- Ruler

- Clear packing tape

- Water

- Optional: food coloring

WHAT TO DO

1 STARTING at the base of the PVC pipe, wrap the clear tubing up the pipe, leaving about ¼ inch (0.6 cm) of the tubing to hang over the base of the pipe. Continue wrapping the tubing up the pipe, leaving about the same amount of space between each spiral.

2 WHEN YOU REACH the top of the pipe, allow about ¾ inch (1.9 cm) of tubing to hang off the top of the pipe. Cut off any excess tubing with the scissors.

3 HOLDING the tubing and pipe as best you can (you may want to ask someone else to help hold or to tape!), wrap the clear packing tape all around the tubing to secure it in place. This is your Archimedes' screw.

4 FILL the bowl with water. To more easily see the water as it moves, add about 10 drops of food coloring to the water and stir it in.

5 PLACE the bottom of your screw into the bowl of water. Place the cup directly below the top of the screw.

6 SLOWLY ROTATE the screw within the water so that it is scooping up the liquid through the tubing.

WHAT'S GOING ON?

As you turn the Archimedes' screw, the bottom end scoops up some water. As the screw turns, water slides along and up the tube. Meanwhile, as you keep turning the screw, more water continues to be scooped into the tube from the bowl. As this happens, it forces the water already in the tube to be pushed higher and higher, until it's eventually pushed out through the top.

THINK ABOUT IT

What do you think would happen if you made your coils tighter? Would it be easier or harder to push the liquid up the Archimedes' screw?

> SOLVE THIS!
> SIMPLE MACHINES

Simple machines make work easier. Take a look at these scenarios, and grab your makerbox. Can you tinker up some simple-machine solutions? Remember there's no right answer!

SITUATION #1

You're in Siberia to study the nerpa, or Baikal seal.

These seals live in a lake far from the ocean. No one knows how they got there! Lake Baikal is very cold, and it freezes over for several months of the year. To study the conditions of the lake, you'd like to drill a hole in the ice. It's important that the hole you make is large enough to take your measurements, but not too large to compromise the integrity of the ice. How can you make a hole in the ice that's just right?

SITUATION #2

For hours after a rainstorm, huge puddles seem to linger in the emu enclosure of your wildlife conservation center.

While the emus seem to enjoy sloshing though the puddles, the rain makes for a very wet and muddy enclosure. Is there a way to divert the rainwater to prevent it from pooling?

SITUATION #3

You're working on an archaeological dig site, and even the tiniest artifact fragment could be valuable to researchers.

As you dig, none of the soil you move is discarded. That's because it's possible some very small but important artifact has been missed! Archaeologists run the soil through filters to find small, overlooked treasures. Can you devise a way to sift through the soil and then move it out of the way?

SITUATION #4

You're about to spend several hours watching birds of paradise, carefully photographing and documenting their behavior from your perch in a treetop.

The photos, sketches, audio recordings, and notes you'll capture will be great additions to your research. Now it's time to start your day, but your first challenge is: How do you get your equipment—and yourself—up the tree?

NOTES

▶ CHAPTER 2

MATERIALS

QUICK FACTS

Have you ever stopped to think about all the **DIFFERENT MATERIALS THAT MAKE UP THE THINGS AROUND YOU?**

Some things are made from natural materials like wood or clay. Other things are made from human-made materials like plastic.

METAL

PLASTIC

WOOD

CERAMIC

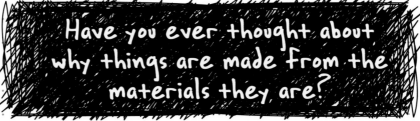

Have you ever thought about why things are made from the materials they are?

GLASS

CLOTH AND RUBBER

PURPOSE & PROPERTIES

IT'S IMPORTANT TO SELECT THE RIGHT MATERIAL FOR THE RIGHT PURPOSE BECAUSE DIFFERENT MATERIALS HAVE DIFFERENT PROPERTIES.

Imagine if your shoes were made out of glass or your backpack was made out of wood. That wouldn't be very useful! Glass is brittle and breaks easily. But fabric is soft, breathable, and comfortable, and rubber bounces well to absorb shocks while you're walking or running.

TRIAL & ERROR

SOMETIMES IT TAKES A LOT OF TRIAL AND ERROR TO FIND THE RIGHT MATERIAL FOR THE JOB.

Sometimes it takes centuries (and also advancements in technology) to get it right, and sometimes some quick experimentation can narrow down the choices. In any case, it helps to understand how different materials behave.

LET'S EXPLORE SOME DIFFERENT MATERIALS.

DIFFICULTY

MINIMUM PEOPLE

POWER COLORS

One easy property of materials to spot is **COLOR.** But color doesn't just make the material look silvery or purple or minty seafoam green. The color may actually affect how the material will behave when it's used in a product. One of the key differences can be seen when comparing dark colors and light colors. Let's take a look.

WHAT YOU'LL NEED

- 2 empty 2-liter soda bottles
- 2 small balloons
- Black paint
- White paint
- A sunny day
- Tape or rubber bands (optional)

WHAT TO DO

1 PAINT one bottle completely black and the other bottle completely white.

2 WHEN the bottles are fully dry, stretch one balloon tightly over each of the two bottles' necks. Make sure both of the balloons are secured tightly in place. If the fit is loose, you may need to tighten them with tape or rubber bands.

3 PLACE both bottles directly in the sun. Come back in 30 minutes to see the results.

TIP! The results will be best if you cool the bottles in an air-conditioned room before placing them in the sun.

WHAT'S GOING ON?

The bottles may seem empty, but don't be fooled. They're actually full of air. When air in the bottles is heated by sunlight, the air expands. Since the bottles were sealed by the balloons, the air has no choice but to expand upward and into the balloon.

The balloon on the bottle painted black should have expanded more than the balloon on the bottle painted white. This is because the color black absorbs sunlight while the color white reflects sunlight. Since the black bottle absorbs the sunlight more than the white bottle, the air in the black bottle heats up much more quickly.

THINK ABOUT IT

What color clothes would you choose to wear on a very warm day?

A ROOF OVER YOUR HEAD

WHY WOULD ANYONE CARE ABOUT THE COLOR OF A ROOF?

The materials a builder selects for the roof of a house, as well as the color of the materials, could have a very big impact on the comfort of its residents. Since the color black absorbs more heat, a black roof will absorb the rays of the sun and heat the home much better than lighter-colored roofs. A black roof might be a good choice for very cold climates, but likely not the best choice for homes built in warmer climates like the desert or tropics.

DIFFICULTY

MINIMUM PEOPLE

RESCUE A DINOSAUR

You've stumbled on a dinosaur preserved in a block of ice. What luck! Imagine all you could learn if you were able to remove the skeleton from its frozen casing. Are you up for the challenge?

WHAT TO DO

1 PLACE one toy in each cup, with ice cubes above and below.

2 FILL both cups of water until the toys are completely submerged.

3 PLACE the cups in the freezer until the water is completely frozen. While your ice is freezing, decide how you will rescue the skeleton. How could you get the ice to melt if you were out in the field?

4 TAKE the cups out of the freezer. Remove the ice blocks from the cups. Now put your plan into action!

Need a hint to get started? Think about how different colors affect heat and energy. Can you put the power of colors to the test?

Can you melt your ice cube faster than the ice would melt on its own?

WHAT'S GOING ON?

What's going on depends on your method! Did you use the power of colors to heat the ice? What role did different materials play? How did it work out?

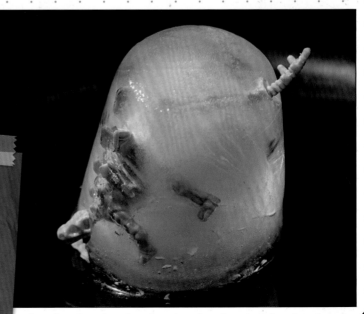

DIFFICULTY

MINIMUM PEOPLE

GRAB AN ADULT!

CLEAN & CLEAR

All living things on Earth need water to survive. And there's plenty of water around: It covers two-thirds of Earth. The problem is, in some parts of the world, water may not be safe for drinking. Chemicals, bacteria, and even small organisms can pollute lakes, rivers, and streams. Drinking polluted water can make people sick.

One of the most basic ways to clean water is with a **FILTER.** You would need a high-tech filter to make water clean enough so that it's safe to drink, but you can clean water yourself so that it's clear enough to use for watering plants! Try it for yourself!

WHAT YOU'LL NEED

- Empty 2-liter soda bottle with its cap

- Scissors

- ½ cup of clean sand

- ½ cup of clean gravel or small pebbles

- ½ cup of clean rocks, bigger than the pebbles

- 2 cotton balls

- A thumbtack or hammer and nail

- Clean empty jar

- Dirty, murky water: If you have access to a pond or creek you can get the water from there, otherwise mixing a little mud, leaves, twigs, and grass with clean tap water works, too.

WHAT TO DO

1 USING THE SCISSORS, carefully remove about 2 inches (5 cm) from the base of the soda bottle. Remember to be safe. You may want an adult to help.

2 CAREFULLY PUSH the thumbtack into the bottle cap. Wiggle it around so that it creates a small hole in the cap. The hole should be about the size of a narrow straw. If the thumbtack doesn't work, ask an adult to use a hammer and nail.

3 PLACE the cap on the soda bottle and screw it closed.

4 PUT the soda bottle upside down, with the cut opening at the top, into the bottom of the bottle. You'll build the filter here before moving it to the empty jar. The jar will be used to trap the clean, filtered, water.

5 NOW YOU'RE READY to build your filter. Take a look at your materials. What properties do they have? Think about how a filter works: Dirty water pours in from the top, and stuff gets trapped as the water makes its way through the layers. By the time the water gets to the bottom, most of the stuff has been filtered out.

6 YOU'LL NEED to work backward, stuffing the material you want to be the last step into the bottle first. Then add the middle layers, then the first layer on top.

7 MOVE your filter (the top half of the bottle) to the empty jar, and slowly pour the dirty water into the top of your filter. Be careful not to pour too quickly so as not to disrupt the layers of the filter.

WHAT'S GOING ON?

Notice the water travels through the layers of your filter by going through a series of barriers. Most filters work by trapping the biggest things first, then smaller and smaller until the bottom layer is capturing just the last bit of the smallest impurities. In this case, you'd want to build your filter so that first the water reaches the larger stones, then the smaller gravel, then the very fine sand, and finally the cotton balls. The first layer of the filter removes larger particles from the water like grass and twigs. As the water makes its way through the filter's layers, smaller and smaller impurities in the water get removed until the water comes out clean. By packing down the layers of the filter as tightly as possible, the water is forced to flow slowly through the filter, but this gives the filter more time to trap the impurities from the water.

When the water begins to slowly drip out of the filter, does it look cleaner than when it went into the filter?

THINK ABOUT IT

What do you think will happen if you changed the order of the filter's layers? Can you think of other materials to select that could be used for the filter?

WARNING

It's important to keep in mind that even though the water looks clean, it is not safe for you or your pets to drink. There may be other harmful things in the water, like bacteria or microorganisms, which are too small to see. Boiling the water is a good way to kill bacteria or microorganisms, but even that may not remove all harmful elements in the water. But you can use your filtered water to feed some thirsty houseplants!

DIFFICULTY

MINIMUM PEOPLE

WALKING WATER

You probably know that if you wear your sneakers to go puddle jumping, they'll probably get wet and soaked through to your socks. That's because many materials **ABSORB,** or soak in, water. But there are also many materials that water does not soak into. These materials are said to repel water.

Understanding *how* water moves through absorbent materials is important, too. If you know how the water moves, then you can better control its movement. That can be handy for everything from transporting water to cleaning up spills. Try it for yourself!

WHAT YOU'LL NEED

- 5 clear plastic cups
- Food coloring in red, yellow, and blue
- Water
- Paper towels

WHAT TO DO

1 FILL three of the cups about three-quarters of the way with water.

2 ADD red food coloring to one cup, yellow to another, and blue to the last cup.

3 PLACE the cups in a straight line in the following sequence from left to right: 1) cup with red liquid, 2) empty cup, 3) cup with yellow liquid, 4) empty cup, 5) cup with blue liquid.

4 TAKE a paper towel square and roll it into a long tube. Place one end in the cup with the red liquid and the other end into the empty cup to the right of it.

5 TAKE another paper towel square and roll it into a long tube. Place one end in the yellow liquid and the other end into the empty cup to the left of it.

6 REPEAT steps 4 and 5, but this time between the cups filled with yellow and blue liquid.

7 AFTER A FEW HOURS, observe the results.

RISE UP!

WE ALL KNOW WE HAVE BLOOD RUNNING THROUGHOUT OUR BODIES. But how is it possible for the blood to stay in the upper parts of our bodies? Wouldn't the blood fall to our feet because of gravity? Lucky for us, blood stays where it needs to stay, and it's all thanks to capillaries. Capillaries behave like little sponges that help absorb blood and carry it where it needs to go.

But it's not just humans who have capillaries. Almost all animals have capillaries to help circulate blood. Even plants have capillaries. Plant capillaries don't transport blood—they carry water and nutrients through their stems to help the plant grow.

WHAT'S GOING ON?

Paper towels are made of a material that is highly absorbent. The water is soaked up by the paper towel and moved into the empty cups. The process where liquid moves up something solid, like a paper towel, is known as capillary action. Capillary action is what makes water move or "walk" up the paper towels and into the empty cup. The empty cup fills up with water until the water levels of all the cups are equal. When red mixes with yellow it makes the color orange. When yellow mixes with blue it makes the color green.

THINK ABOUT IT

What if you tried this experiment with other materials, like old socks, instead of paper towels? What if instead of water you used other liquids, like vinegar or oil? Do you think you would get similar results?

The materials you choose can have lots of effects on the final product. Take a look at these scenarios, then grab your makerbox. Can you tinker up some solutions using the best materials? Remember, there's no right answer!

SITUATION #1

You're a biologist tracking a family of mountain gorillas in central Africa.

So far, everything's going great. There's just one problem. Mosquitoes bother you all day and now you're itchy all the time. How can you protect yourself from mosquitoes without disturbing the gorillas while you observe them?

You're a brand—new nature photographer on your very first assignment in the Arctic.

You're hoping to snap pictures of polar bears in their natural habitat, but you must stay hidden to avoid attracting the polar bears' attention. What kind of outfit can you devise to blend with the snow and ice yet keep you warm in the subfreezing temperatures?

SITUATION #3

You're a botanist trying to understand why a farm's crops are not thriving, even though the farmers insist they are watering the fields every day.

You take a look at the soil the crops are planted in. It's dry, and the soil particles are large. Soil that contains larger particles has a hard time absorbing water because water passes too quickly through the larger gaps. How can you improve the flow of water to the crops?

SITUATION #4

You're a scientist working in the Amazon rain forest studying the interaction between plants, animals, and the environment.

Your field work requires a lot of equipment to help you collect samples and measure data. There's one big problem: The lab equipment isn't waterproof, and here in the rain forest, frequent rainstorms are a good bet. What kind of canopy can you devise to help keep your equipment dry while diverting rainwater away from your work area?

▶ CHAPTER 3

SYSTEMS

QUICK FACTS

A SYSTEM IS A SET OF CONNECTED PARTS THAT WORK TOGETHER TO DO A JOB.

There are systems all around you. For example, a bicycle can be thought of as a system. It is made of many parts, like the wheels, gears, breaks, handlebar, and frame. All these parts connect to form the bicycle system.

CONNECTION

FOR A SYSTEM TO OPERATE PROPERLY, ALL OF ITS PARTS MUST BE CONNECTED IN JUST THE RIGHT WAY.

If one part of the bicycle system is changed, the entire bicycle changes. Imagine what happens if one of the bicycle's tires deflates. The bicycle wouldn't work. What if the bicycle's frame becomes bent? It would make the bicycle difficult to ride.

CAUSE & EFFECT

WITH ALL OF THOSE INTERCONNECTED PARTS, SYSTEMS OFTEN RELY ON CAUSE-AND-EFFECT RELATIONSHIPS.

For example, because you push the pedals on your bike, they rotate. Because they rotate, they cause the gears to rotate. Because the gears rotate, they cause the chain to rotate. Because the chain rotates, the wheels rotate. And because the wheels rotate, off you go!

PEDAL rotation

causes

GEAR rotation

causes

CHAIN rotation

WHEEL rotation

causes

LET'S EXPLORE SOME DIFFERENT SYSTEMS.

DIFFICULTY

MINIMUM PEOPLE

WATER FROM LEAVES

Trees may look like they're just standing and growing right there in the ground all on their own. But believe it or not, trees are a kind of system—they need to **INTERACT WITH THEIR SURROUNDINGS,** taking in and releasing matter, in order to survive. To grow, trees must absorb water and nutrients from the soil. Trees also release matter back out into their surroundings, like oxygen and water vapor. You can see it in action!

WHAT YOU'LL NEED

- A clean, clear plastic bag
- String
- A tree with large green leaves
- A sunny day

WHAT TO DO

1 CHOOSE a branch on the tree with a large number of healthy-looking leaves, preferably in direct sunlight.

2 PLACE the plastic bag over the leaves and secure it very tightly with the string.

3 CHECK your bag every hour for collected water.

NOTE! Depending on the type of tree and the amount of sunlight, it could take several hours to see results.

WHAT'S GOING ON?

It's an invisible process, but water is always evaporating from leaves. Plants get water from the soil through their roots. This water is transported through the plant, to help the plant live and grow. But some of this water may evaporate through small pores on the underside of leaves called stoma. This process is called transpiration. It's like the tree is sweating! Usually, the leaves transpire water into the air, but in this experiment, the plastic bag traps and collects the water.

THINK ABOUT IT

Since transpiration depends on sunlight, do you think you would collect the same amount of water in the evening? Why or why not?

 WARNING It's important not to drink the water that collects in the bag. The water may not be clean to drink. It's a great idea to return the water into the system by watering the soil beneath the tree.

BREAK A SWEAT

AN ACRE (0.4 HA) OF CORN CAN TRANSPIRE UP TO 400,000 GALLONS (1.5 MILLION L) OF WATER IN ONE GROWING SEASON!

But there are many factors that affect how much plants transpire. On very hot days, transpiration rates increase. This is because the warmer temperatures cause the stoma to open wider, allowing more water to escape from the leaves. This is similar to how humans sweat more on very hot days. Some plants, especially plants that grow in dry, desert climates like cacti, barely transpire at all. Since water is scarce in their environment, they need to hold on to as much water as they can to survive.

DIFFICULTY

MINIMUM PEOPLE

GRAB AN ADULT!

MARBLE MAZE CHALLENGE

Thinking about a system means thinking about how all the parts work together and what each part causes another part to do. Look at the **CAUSE-AND-EFFECT RELATIONSHIPS** within the system. Ask yourself: Which parts connect to which other parts? Does each connect to just one or to more than one? What happens to Part B when Part A is activated?

WHAT YOU'LL NEED

- Shoebox

- Marble

- Other materials to build a maze, such as straws, beads, chopsticks, mini blocks, spools, glue, and tape

One easy way to explore cause and effect is a marble maze. In a marble maze, the player (you) must tilt a box to make the marble roll. You'll need to roll the marble around obstacles from its start line to its finish. To do that, you'll need to think about what direction to tip the box, how much to tilt it, and how to use the obstacles to change the direction of the marble as needed. It can take a lot of trial and error, and a lot of asking yourself: If I do ____, what will happen to my marble?

Building a marble maze is even more complex. Not only do you need to figure out how to get your marble from start to finish, you'll need to figure out where the start and finish *are* and how the marble *should* travel. Try it for yourself!

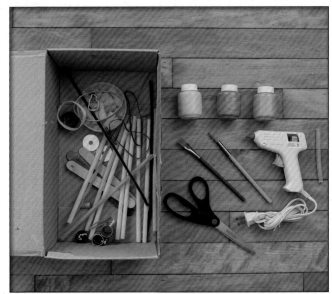

WHAT TO DO

THINK about the system you are designing. Your goal is to make a path that you can roll a marble through from the start of the maze to the end of the maze. You'll do this by gluing or taping your materials into the box to form the path. For more fun, glue in some objects that will be obstacles for your marble. You'll have to work to roll the ball around them! Want to make it a super-challenging maze? Try adding a few different possible paths from the start to the finish.

1 MARK one spot of the maze as "start" and another as "finish." Your spots can be anywhere in the box.

2 NOW MAKE A PATH from the start point to the finish point. Remember, you'll need to guide your marble to roll along the path by tilting the box, so be sure to only leave a space between materials where you want a challenging hole for your marble to have to pass across.

3 REARRANGE the materials in the box as many times as you want until you're happy with your path.

4 WHEN you're satisfied with how the maze is laid out, use glue or tape to secure the maze parts in place.

5 PLACE the marble at the maze's start and give it a whirl! Tilt the box in different directions to see if you can get your marble from the start point to the finish point.

53

DIFFICULTY

MINIMUM PEOPLE

RAIN FOREST IN A BOTTLE

An **ECOSYSTEM** is a system where all living things in a given area work together and interact with their environment. The rain forest is one of the most diverse and complicated ecosystems on our planet. A rain forest functions best as a self-contained system. That's where one part of the system influences the other parts of the system in perfect balance, without outside influences. Try it for yourself!

WHAT YOU'LL NEED

- 1 clean, clear, airtight container (like a large mason jar)

- Clean gravel or rocks (If you get them from outside, be sure to wash them off.)

- Activated charcoal (You can buy this from a pet store.)

- Potting soil

- 1 or 2 small plants (Tropical ones, such as ferns, are a great choice.)

- Decorative items like rocks, figurines, or wood (optional)

- Water

WHAT TO DO

1 **PLACE** a layer of gravel into the jar, about 2 inches (5 cm) deep. This layer provides drainage for excess water.

2 **POUR** about an inch (2.5 cm) of activated charcoal on top of the gravel. The charcoal is useful because it helps keep the system clean.

3 **ADD** about 4 inches (10 cm) of soil.

4 **MAKE** a small hole in the soil using your finger. Carefully remove the plant you've chosen from its container. Take care to handle the plant's roots delicately. Place the plant into the hole, and then fill in the hole with soil. If using more than one plant, repeat this step, making sure there is some distance between plants.

5 **IF YOU WANT** to decorate your rain forest scene, place your figurines inside the container.

6 **ADD** a small amount of water to the soil. The soil should be damp but not drenched.

7 **SEAL** the container. Place it near a window, but not in direct sunlight. If the container receives too much sunlight it will get too hot for the plant.

TIP! Make sure the jar you are using is very clean. This will prevent bacteria or mold growth and will keep your rain forest ecosystem healthy.

THINK ABOUT IT

What would happen to your rain forest if you opened it frequently? Do you think the self-contained system would grow better or worse over time with frequent contact to the outside air? Why or why not?

WHAT'S GOING ON?

Your tiny rain forest is a closed ecosystem. Moisture in your rain forest evaporates from the soil and the plant leaves. This moisture condenses on the container walls, forming water droplets. These water droplets then "rain," falling back down to the soil. This cycle repeats over and over again. As long as the container stays sealed and the ecosystem stays healthy, the cycle will continue for months. No need to add more water! For the first few days, you may notice that the container appears cloudy. This is perfectly normal! In a few days, the cloud will be replaced by water droplets.

DIFFICULTY

MINIMUM PEOPLE

RUBE GOLDBERG MACHINE

A Rube Goldberg machine is a system that links a series of tasks, one task causing another, to form a **CHAIN REACTION.** To understand how a chain reaction works, imagine dominoes lined up in a row. When the first domino falls, it knocks over the next domino, and so on until all of the dominoes have fallen. A Rube Goldberg machine works similarly: One part of the system triggers the next part and so on in a silly (and completely unnecessary) chain reaction to accomplish a simple task. The catch, though, is that just like in any other system, each step of a Rube Goldberg machine needs to happen just right in order to cause the next step to fire. So instead of using a napkin the boring way, a Rube Goldberg machine would be an entire wacky face-wiping contraption!

Rube Goldberg's Self–Operating Napkin

Start by lifting a soup spoon (A) that pulls a string (B) that jerks a ladle (C) that then throws a cracker (D) past a parrot (E). When the parrot jumps for the cracker, its perch (F) tilts and drops seeds (G) into a pail (H). The extra weight in the pail pulls a cord (I) that opens and lights an automatic lighter (J), which sets off a rocket (K) that causes a sickle (L) to cut a string (M) that allows a pendulum with a napkin attached to it (N) to swing back and forth to wipe the chin.

THE MAN BEHIND THE MACHINE

THE RUBE GOLDBERG MACHINE WAS NAMED AFTER REUBEN "RUBE" GOLDBERG. He was best known for his popular cartoons that depicted complicated gadgets that perform simple tasks.

Ready to create a Rube Goldberg machine of your own? Your mission: Pop a balloon with a pin. Sounds easy, right? All you have to do is touch the pin to the balloon and it pops. Not so fast! For this challenge, you must design a multistep system to accomplish the task. For added fun, grab a few friends or family members to try the challenge as well.

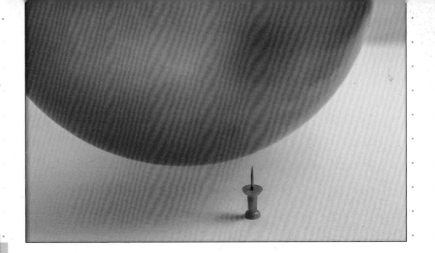

WHAT YOU'LL NEED

- 1 inflated balloon

- 1 pushpin

- Other materials to build a chain reaction. A few materials to consider: paper towel tubes, marbles, ramps, or strings. Use your imagination!

WHAT TO DO

1 **EXAMINE** your materials. What parts do they have? How do they behave? What do they do? What causes them to do what they do?

2 **THINK** about a sequence of events and a possible chain reaction. Draw your ideas on paper.

3 **TEST** each of the steps and observe the results.

4 **AS YOU TEST** each step, adjust the chain reaction so you get the desired result. Consider the order of your steps. Would it make sense to swap any?

5 **KEEP** building on your chain reaction until you have a sequence of steps that will pop the balloon with a pin.

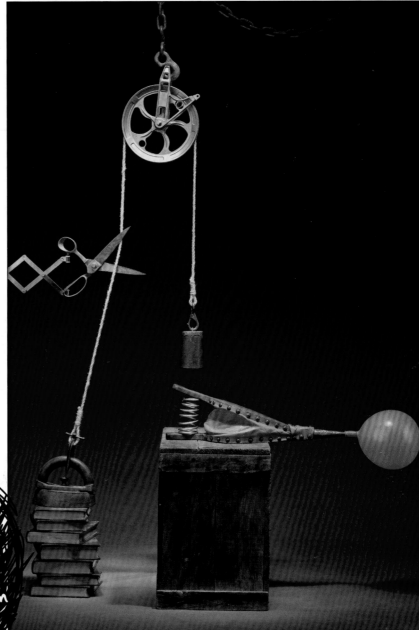

The more steps in your system, the harder it will be to pop the balloon. Can you design a system with at least three steps before the balloon pops? How about five?

> # SOLVE THIS!
> ## > SYSTEMS

Systems are every-where! Take a look at these scenarios, then grab your makerbox. Can you tinker up some solutions that take advantage of how parts within a system interact? Remember, there's no right answer!

SITUATION #1

You're on a mountain expedition. You and your expedition team make camp for the night and build a fire.

It's been a long day of trekking, and you're exhausted. You'll be famished come morning, so it would be great to have a warm breakfast waiting for you when you get up. You know how dangerous it is to let a fire burn overnight, though. How can you ensure you have breakfast ready when you wake, even with safely putting out the campfire for the night?

SITUATION #2

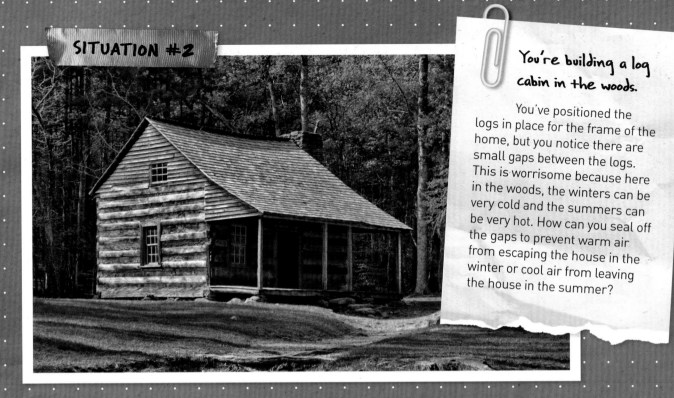

You're building a log cabin in the woods.

You've positioned the logs in place for the frame of the home, but you notice there are small gaps between the logs. This is worrisome because here in the woods, the winters can be very cold and the summers can be very hot. How can you seal off the gaps to prevent warm air from escaping the house in the winter or cool air from leaving the house in the summer?

SITUATION #3

As a conservationist, you've been asked to give a talk about rain forest deforestation to a gathering of political leaders.

You want to explain why deforestation has a dangerous impact on the ecosystem. What model could you build to explain to your audience that deforestation has consequences that might set off a chain reaction of harmful events?

SITUATION #4

You're an entomologist studying the bee population in a small town.

Folks in the area tell you they have noticed a sharp decline in the bee population. They're worried about the effect this will have on the plants in the area. Without bees to pollinate them, many of the plants cannot grow. You look around and see that many new buildings have been built in the area. You think this may be affecting the bees' ability to find the flowers they need. How can you help the community find ways to help the bees?

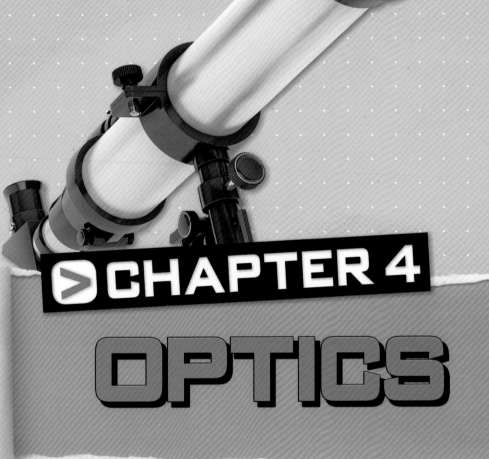

► CHAPTER 4

OPTICS

QUICK FACTS

LIGHT IS A FORM OF ENERGY that lets you see a reflection in a mirror, a rainbow in the sky, an image on a computer screen, and your puppy doing tricks in the backyard.

Earth's main source of light is THE SUN, but light also comes from human-made sources like LAMPS, LIGHTBULBS, FLASHLIGHTS, AND FIRES.

REFLECTION

WITHOUT LIGHT, WE WOULDN'T BE ABLE TO SEE ANYTHING. THAT'S BECAUSE OF WHAT REALLY HAPPENS WHEN YOU SEE AN OBJECT:

Light hits the object, then bounces back to travel to our eyes. So, technically, you're not seeing the actual object. You're looking at a reflection of the object. If you were to completely eliminate the source of light, the object would look like it had disappeared.

COLORS

LIGHT IS USUALLY THOUGHT OF AS WHITE, BUT THAT'S NOT QUITE TRUE.

White light actually contains every single color mixed together. Why do the leaves of a tree appear green, then? When light shines on the tree, the leaves reflect only the green part of light. The leaves absorb all the other colors. Since only green light is reflected, it's this green light that hits our eyes, making us see the leaf as green.

LET'S EXPLORE THE SCIENCE OF LIGHT AND HOW WE SEE.

DIFFICULTY

MINIMUM PEOPLE

REFLECTION TARGET PRACTICE

LIGHT travels 186,000 miles a second (almost 300,000 km/s). That's really fast! (Actually, it's faster than anything else in the universe!) In one second, light can travel the distance around Earth seven times.

But light always travels in a straight line … unless something gets in its way. One way to change the direction of light is to have it bounce off a shiny surface, like metal or mirrors. Try it for yourself!

WHAT YOU'LL NEED

- Flashlight

- Handheld mirror

- Sheet of black paper

- Tape

- A friend

WHAT TO DO

1 **SELECT** a space for this activity. A room where you can dim the lights or close the window shades is a great choice. This activity works best when the room isn't too big or too bright. Try flashing your flashlight against the walls in the space you've selected to make sure the beam is visible. As long as you can see the light from the flashlight you're good to go! If you can't see the light beam, try moving closer to the wall.

2 **ASK** your friend to tape the sheet of black paper to one of the walls in the room. This will be your target.

3 **TURN** the flashlight on and point it at the target. Notice how the beam of light from the flashlight travels in a straight line.

4 **TURN OFF** the flashlight. Ask your friend to stand or sit in a spot between you and the target on the wall (without blocking the target) and hold the mirror with the reflective side facing outward at any angle. You, your friend, and the target should make a triangle.

5 **POINT** the flashlight, without turning it on, at the mirror. Try to predict where the beam of light will go. Will it hit your target?

6 **NOW,** while still pointing the flashlight at the mirror, turn the flashlight on. Notice how the beam of light travels. Was your prediction correct?

7 **ASK** your friend to shift the mirror from side to side or up and down to change the angle of the beam of light until it hits the target.

6

WHAT'S GOING ON?

Mirrored surfaces have a special effect on light. The surface is highly reflective, which means almost none of the light that hits a mirror is absorbed by the mirror. Instead, the mirror causes nearly all of the light that hits it to bounce off of it. When you stand in front of a mirror, light bounces off of you, hits the mirror, and bounces into your eyes—and voilà! An image of you.

THINK ABOUT IT

You may have seen your reflection against a shiny metal pot or against the metal surface of a car. You might even see your reflection on the surface of water if the water is very still. Why do you think that is? What do all of these surfaces have in common that allow you to see your reflection?

MIRROR ON THE MOON

IN 1969, APOLLO 11 ASTRONAUTS BUZZ ALDRIN AND NEIL ARMSTRONG DID MORE THAN JUST WALK ON THE MOON. They left something behind: A mirror! The mirror on the moon is used for important scientific research. When it is struck by a laser beam, the mirror reflects that beam back to its source. Astronomers measure how long it takes for the laser beam to come back to Earth. Using this information, astronomers have been able to determine that the moon is slowly drifting away from Earth.

COLOR KALEIDOSCOPE

KALEIDOSCOPES are toys that make beautiful, mesmerizing images. Each turn of the kaleidoscope creates a brand-new pattern. The interesting thing about kaleidoscopes is that all of the patterns produced are perfectly symmetrical. This symmetry is created by mirrors carefully arranged within the kaleidoscope. As you look through the viewer and rotate the kaleidoscope, the mirrors within reflect the movement of small objects. Try it for yourself!

WHAT YOU'LL NEED

- Empty paper towel tube

- Permanent marker with a thin tip

- Ruler

- Multicolored translucent beads

- Tape

- Glue

- Hot glue

- Clear plastic fruit containers—for example, the clear plastic clamshell-style containers strawberries and blueberries are often sold in

- Scissors

- Aluminum foil

- Letter-size sheet of card stock paper

WHAT TO DO

1 PLACE the paper towel tube on top of the clear plastic container. Using the marker, trace around the paper towel tube. Then cut out the circle you traced with the scissors.

2 REPEAT step one so you have a second plastic circle.

3 TRIM both of the plastic circles so they fit just inside the paper towel tube.

4 SLIDE one of the plastic circles into the tube, just slightly below the rim. Ask an adult to place hot glue around the edge of the circle to secure it in place.

5 ONCE the glue is dry, place the tube on its end, with the plastic circle closest to you. Place beads inside the tube so they rest atop the plastic circle.

6 PLACE the second plastic circle on the end of the tube so that the beads are trapped between the two pieces of plastic. Ask an adult to glue on the circle.

7 TAKE the sheet of card stock paper and spread glue across it. Measure a sheet of aluminum foil to be approximately the size of the sheet of card stock. Don't worry if it's not exact! Glue the aluminum foil to the card stock paper. Repeat on the other side.

8 PLACE the ruler into the tube and measure the distance between the inner plastic circle and the open top of the paper towel tube. Cut your foil-covered card stock to be that length.

9 DIVIDE the card stock into three equal strips, by drawing straight lines (use the ruler to help you). Each strip should measure 1 inch (2.5 cm) wide.

10 FOLD the card stock along the lines to form a triangle. Tape the edges together to keep it in place.

11 INSERT the cardboard triangle into the tube.

12 POINT the kaleidoscope toward a light. Look through the triangle piece you inserted in the previous step. Turn it and see what happens.

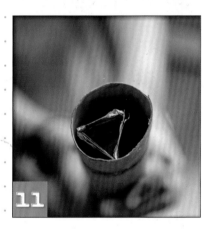

WHAT'S GOING ON?

When you turn the kaleidoscope, the beads inside shift. As you look through the kaleidoscope's viewer, the aluminum foil acts like a mirror, reflecting the positions of the beads. Because there are three mirrors facing each other, they reflect back and forth, causing the detailed patterns you see.

THINK ABOUT IT

Do you think your kaleidoscope would work differently if you didn't point it toward the light? Try it!

DIFFICULTY

MINIMUM PEOPLE

GRAB AN ADULT!

SCOPING THE SCENE

If you want to see an object, it needs to be in your line of sight. You can't see through an obstacle or around a wall, right? Well, you can with the help of a special tool called a periscope! A periscope brings what is around corners, over walls, or beyond your line of sight into view. It's super useful for sleuthing.

PERISCOPES work by using mirrors to bounce light from one place to another. A typical periscope uses two mirrors. When light falls against the first mirror it is reflected onto the second mirror. The light then bounces again, but this time it reflects into the observer's eye. Try it for yourself!

WHAT YOU'LL NEED

- 2 empty 1-quart milk cartons, cleaned and dried

- 2 small pocket mirrors (Thin, flat, square mirrors work best, but other mirrors work as well.)

- Scissors

- Ruler

- Pen

- Masking tape

RISING ABOVE THE CROWD

JOHANNES GUTENBERG, WHO LIVED IN THE 15TH CENTURY, is perhaps best known for his invention of the movable-type printing press. But Gutenberg also invented a solution to another important problem. During his time, there was a big festival in the town of Aachen, Germany. The town was jam-packed with crowds. So Gutenberg invented a periscope to allow people to see the festivities over the heads of other festival-goers!

WHAT TO DO

1 USE the scissors to carefully cut and remove the pointed top of each milk carton.

2 SET one milk carton aside. Hold the other milk carton with the opening at the top. On one side of the carton, measure ¼ inch (0.6 cm) from the bottom, the left edge, and the right edge of the milk carton, making a small mark at each measure point. Draw lines connecting each of the three marks, then a fourth line to make a square. Then cut the square hole from the side of the carton.

3 PUT the milk carton on its side and turn it so the hole you just cut is facing your right. On the side that is facing up, use the ruler to measure 3 inches (7.6 cm) from the bottom (on the left edge) of the container. Use the pen to make a mark there. Next, use your ruler to draw a straight, diagonal line from the mark you just made to the bottom right corner.

4 MEASURE the length of one of your mirrors. Use the scissors to cut a slit the length of the mirror along the line you just made. Be sure to not cut all the way to the edges of the milk carton.

5 SLIDE the mirror through the slit you just made so the reflecting side of the mirror faces the hole in the carton.

6 SECURE the mirror in place with the masking tape.

7 HOLD the carton with the open end facing up. Look through the hole you cut in your carton. Do you see your ceiling? If not, adjust the mirror and re-tape it in place.

8 REPEAT steps 2 through 7 with the second milk carton.

9 STAND one carton on a table with the hole facing you. Stand the other carton upside down with the mirror on top and hole facing away from you.

10 SQUEEZE the bottom of the upside-down carton slightly so it can slide into the other carton.

11 USE the masking tape to secure the two cartons together.

12 USE your periscope to see over and around obstacles!

WHAT'S GOING ON?

The mirrors in the periscope help "bounce" an image that is outside of your line of sight to your eye. This is because mirrors reflect light. In your periscope, light hits the top mirror and bounces to the bottom mirror. It then bounces off the bottom mirror right into your eye!

ALL THE COLORS OF THE RAINBOW

With tools called **SPECTROSCOPES** and **PRISMS,** you can separate white light into its components and see all the different colors of the rainbow. A prism is a medium, such as glass, that bends all the different wave lengths of light as they enter the medium. Each wavelength bends differently and leaves the prism at a different angle, separating the light and creating a rainbow. This is called refraction. Refraction happens when light passes from one medium—in this case, air—to another medium—in this case, glass. Spectroscopes also separate light, but instead of bending light as it passes through a medium, spectroscopes bend light as it passes through an opening or around a barrier. This bending is called diffraction. Try it for yourself!

WHAT YOU'LL NEED

- 1 empty paper towel tube

- Scissors

- Ruler

- Blank or old CD

- Pencil

- Small piece of cardboard

- Tape

WHAT TO DO

1 MEASURE 3 inches (approximately 7.6 cm) up from the end of the paper towel tube and mark it with a pencil. From that mark, draw an upside-down U. The U should go about halfway around the tube. Using the scissors, cut a thin slit along the mark you drew.

2 ON THE OPPOSITE SIDE of the tube, directly across from the slit made in the previous step, use the scissors to cut a small square, approximately 1 inch (2.5 cm) on each side. This is your eyehole.

3 PLACE the paper towel tube on top of the cardboard. Using the pencil, trace around the paper towel tube. Then cut out the circle you traced with the scissors.

4 CUT a small rectangle, approximately ½ inch (1.3 cm) in the center of the cardboard circle, making sure to leave equal space along the top and bottom of the circle.

5 TAPE the cardboard circle to the top of the paper towel tube.

6 INSERT the CD into the slit with the shiny side facing up.

7 TAKE your spectroscope outside. Point the top at the sky, but be sure not to point it directly at the sun. Place your eye against the eyehole. What do you see?

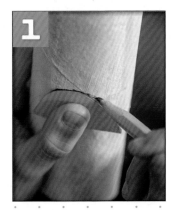

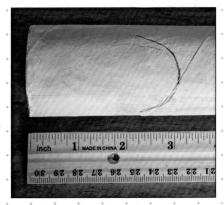

DIFFRACTION MAGIC

IF YOU'VE EVER SEEN BUTTERFLIES, YOU'VE PROBABLY NOTICED THEIR BEAUTIFUL, BRIGHT, SHINY WINGS. Believe it or not, these colors aren't created by pigments in the butterfly's wings. They're an optical illusion! The shiny, iridescent colors come from tiny bumps and grooves on butterflies' wings that cause diffraction. Instead of absorbing certain wavelengths, butterfly wings diffract incoming light. Depending on the pattern of the wings' scales, multiple diffracted light beams bounce off the wings and interfere with one another. This causes certain colors to cancel out and other colors to intensify. When the butterfly flies, its wings appear to change color constantly. As the butterfly moves its wings up and down during flight, it may even, momentarily, seem to disappear and then reappear a short distance away. Some scientists believe butterflies use this trick of light as camouflage from predators.

WHAT'S GOING ON?

Even though a CD looks perfectly flat and smooth, if you look at the surface of the CD under a microscope, you might see bumps and grooves on its surface. These bumps and grooves cause light hitting the CD to diffract—the light waves encounter the bumps and grooves and are forced to shift directions. Different wavelengths will diffract at different angles, causing the light to separate into its components.

THINK ABOUT IT

What do you think will happen if you try your spectroscope with other light sources like flashlights or lightbulbs? Try it! Did you get different results?

TINY THINGS

You may have noticed that when you put a spoon into a glass of water, the spoon appears to bend at the surface of the water. The spoon isn't actually bending. It's the light that is bending as it travels from the air into the water. To help understand how this works, imagine you're running down a boardwalk toward the beach. Your legs are moving at a steady pace, carrying you to the sand, but the moment you actually reach the beach, your speed slows down. This is because the sand provides some resistance against your movement. It's harder for your legs to move through sand than it is across the hard wood of the boardwalk.

The exact same thing happens when light travels through air and into water. The light travels very quickly through air, but the moment it hits water, it slows down. That causes the light to change direction. Light slowing down as it enters the water is what causes the spoon to appear bent.

Compound Microscope

A simple microscope uses a single lens to magnify an object. But the microscopes that most students use in schools are called "compound microscopes" because they use two lenses instead of one.

IN AND OUT

THIS BENDING OF LIGHT IS CALLED REFRACTION.
Lenses are special pieces of glass or plastic that are designed to refract light to help people see objects better. A convex lens bends light inward, making an object appear larger or closer than it is. A concave lens bends rays outward, making an object appear smaller or farther than it is.

MICROSCOPES use lenses and the refraction of light to let you see things too small to see with just your eyes. But you don't need a lens to see refraction at work. You can accomplish the same type of refraction with water. Try it for yourself!

WHAT YOU'LL NEED

- A clear plastic cup

- Plastic wrap

- A rubber band

- Water

- Some interesting objects to observe. Twigs, leaves, or flowers that you find on the ground are great choices. You can also use small objects around the house with tiny details.

WHAT TO DO

1 **PLACE** your object at the bottom of your empty cup.

2 **STRETCH** a piece of plastic wrap over the top of your cup and secure it with a rubber band.

3 **POUR** a small amount of water (a few drops should do it) on top of the plastic wrap. Allow the water to form a small pool.

4 **CLOSE** one eye, and place the other eye over the pool of water. Observe your object through the water.

WHAT'S GOING ON?

Look carefully at the pool of water you used for your microscope. The surface of the water is dome shaped. This curvature makes the water act like a convex lens, bending the light inward and causing the object beneath it to appear bigger than it is. This allows you to observe the tiny details of your object.

THINK ABOUT IT

What do you think will happen if you used more water? (Hint: Will the curvature of the water increase or decrease?)

ZOOM OUT

GRAB AN ADULT!

While microscopes help us see things that are nearby but very small, **TELESCOPES** help us see things that are far away but very large. In other words, telescopes work by making objects that are far away appear closer.

Telescopes work by "gathering light," which helps the human eye believe that an object is closer than it really is. There are two types of telescopes. Reflecting telescopes use mirrors to help direct the light. Refracting telescopes, like the one you'll make, use lenses to capture the light. Try it for yourself!

WHAT YOU'LL NEED

- 2 empty paper towel tubes

- Scissors

- Masking tape

- 2 convex lenses. If an adult you know has old reading glasses they are no longer using, ask them to help you remove the lenses from the frame. Make sure the glasses are reading glasses and not glasses for helping to see things far away. Only reading glasses use convex lenses. If you don't have old reading glasses to use, you can pick some up at most convenience or grocery stores.

1 CUT one of your paper towel tubes lengthwise (all the way up the side). Tuck one edge of the cut side slightly under the other and hold it in place with one hand.

2 INSERT the cut tube into the other paper towel tube. Let go of the inner tube so that it can expand inside the outer tube. The inner tube should now fit snugly into the outer tube, but still be able to slide in and out. If the inner tube is not sliding smoothly, adjust its size. Remove the inner tube and wrap the edge slightly tighter. Then, reinsert the inner tube into the other paper towel tube until it fits just right.

3 USING MASKING TAPE, secure one lens to the outer edge of the inner tube. The curve of the lens should be facing the inside of the tube.

4 THEN, SECURE the second lens to the edge of the outer tube, with the curve of the lens pointing outside of the tube. It's okay if your lenses are bigger than the tube. Try to only tape around the rim of the lenses so you don't cover too much.

5 PLACE your eye against the lens of the inner tube. Aim your telescope at something far away (never use a telescope to look at the sun). Focus by sliding the inner tube in and out until the image becomes clear.

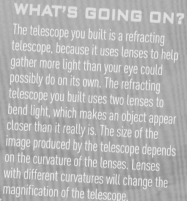

THINK ABOUT IT

Telescopes work by gathering light. Can you think of ways to improve your telescope by helping it gather more light?

WHAT'S GOING ON?

The telescope you built is a refracting telescope, because it uses lenses to help gather more light than your eye could possibly do on its own. The refracting telescope you built uses two lenses to bend light, which makes an object appear closer than it really is. The size of the image produced by the telescope depends on the curvature of the lenses. Lenses with different curvatures will change the magnification of the telescope.

FAR-SEEING

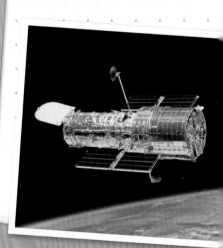

THE HUBBLE SPACE TELESCOPE IS PROBABLY ONE OF THE MOST FAMOUS TELESCOPES EVER INVENTED.

What makes the Hubble Space Telescope so special is that it's actually in space, orbiting Earth. It takes pictures of planets, stars, and galaxies and then transmits images back to Earth. These pictures are very detailed and provide a lot more information than telescopes here on Earth could ever capture. This is because a telescope that sits on Earth is surrounded by the planet's atmosphere, which blocks some of the light coming from space, making the images less precise. —

Optics are all about light and how we see. Take a look at these scenarios, then grab your makerbox. Can you tinker up some enlightening solutions? Remember, there's no right answer!

SITUATION #1

As you hike through twisty caves in mountains, you realize spelunking can be dangerous.

Luckily, as a skilled explorer, you've brought all the necessary safety gear along with you. Like all light, your headlamp beam travels in a straight line. Can you use items you have with you in the cave to build a way to spread the light out to see more of the cave?

SITUATION #2

You're a wildlife biologist studying Africa's lion population.

You want to know more about how they behave in their prides, but you know that the presence of a human often changes their behavior. You would like to photograph the lions from afar to support your studies, but your camera lens can't zoom in close enough. Can you rig a lens extender to photograph the lions safely without getting too close?

SITUATION #3

You're an entomologist looking for unknown insects in the forest.

Suddenly you spot a tiny insect that you think might be new to science. You don't want to remove the insect from its natural habitat, so taking it back to the lab is out of the question. How can you make detailed observations about the insect while you're in the forest so that you can research more about it when you get back to your lab?

SITUATION #4

You're out for a day of birding with your friend, on the lookout for the elusive Siberian accentor.

It's been spotted by other bird-watchers, and you're hoping to catch a glimpse of it, too. Your friend is farther down the path when ... you spot it! The accentor! You want to call out to your friend, but shouting will likely scare the bird away. How can you get your friend's attention using what you have with you?

CHAPTER 5

ENERGY

QUICK FACTS

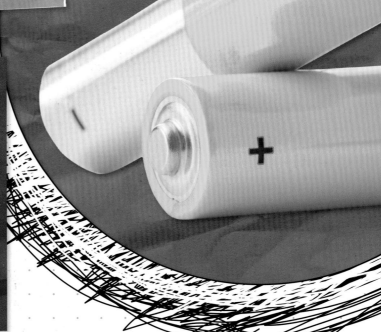

Energy is everywhere. Without it, a tree couldn't grow, a car couldn't drive, and a fire couldn't burn. **ENERGY, PUT SIMPLY, IS WHAT MAKES THE UNIVERSE WORK.** Energy can come from many different sources:

NONRENEWABLE ENERGY

NONRENEWABLE ENERGY COMES FROM SOURCES THAT DEPLETE NATURAL RESOURCES AS THEY ARE USED.

Once the energy source runs out, it cannot be replaced. Examples of nonrenewable energy sources include crude oil, natural gas, and coal.

GASOLINE FROM OIL

COAL

RENEWABLE ENERGY

RENEWABLE ENERGY COMES FROM ENERGY SOURCES THAT WE CAN TAP OVER AND OVER AGAIN.

Sources like the sun and the wind provide renewable energy. We don't run out of sunlight or wind, even if we use it to power our homes and machines. There are several sources of renewable energy.

SOLAR

HYDROPOWER

WIND

GEOTHERMAL

BIOMASS

LET'S EXPLORE WAYS WE CAN USE ENERGY TO MAKE THINGS HAPPEN.

DIFFICULTY

MINIMUM PEOPLE

GRAB AN ADULT!

PORTABLE POWER

A **BATTERY** provides us with portable energy by converting its stored chemical energy into a form of electrical energy. There are three main parts of a battery: The anode (-), the cathode (+), and the electrolyte (a liquid between the + and -). When a battery is in use, a chemical reaction happens inside the battery. This reaction makes a bunch of electrons gather at the anode. But electrons repel each other, causing them to try to move toward the cathode, where there are fewer electrons. However, the electrolyte between the anode and the cathode blocks the electrons from traveling directly between the two sides of the battery. That causes the electrons to build up at the anode. The imbalance of electrons between the two sides creates an electrical charge. The electrons' only outlet is to travel through an outside path (like a wire) that connects the anode to the cathode. Try it for yourself!

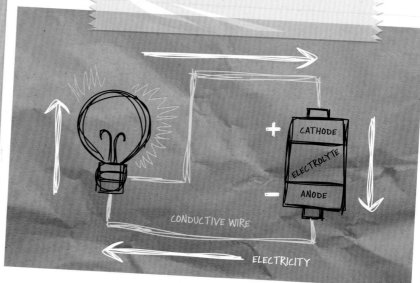

CONDUCTIVE WIRE

ELECTRICITY

CATHODE

ELECTROLYTE

ANODE

Connecting the Dots

When a wire is placed between an anode and cathode, the electrons move through the wire, producing an electric current. This is called a circuit. A circuit is a path that electricity flows along. It starts at the battery, flows through a wire to a lightbulb, clock, calculator, or other object, and back to the other side of the battery. A circuit brings electrical power to any device placed along its path.

POWER PLANT

UNLESS ELECTRONS ARE FLOWING FROM THE ANODE TO THE CATHODE, the chemical reaction does not take place, and none of the battery's power is consumed. This is why a battery can sit on a shelf for a long time and still have power when you finally use it. However, as the battery gets used over time, the chemical process that occurs within the battery changes the anode and the cathode. Eventually, electrons are no longer produced, and the battery dies.

WHAT YOU'LL NEED

- ¼ cup (60 mL) of vinegar

- 1 tablespoon (15 mL) salt

- A bowl

- 4 pennies and 4 nickels

- Dish soap

- Small strip of aluminum foil, about the width of a nickel

- Scissors

- Paper towels or a sheet of printer paper

- LED lightbulb with its wires

WHAT TO DO

1 **MIX** the vinegar and salt in the bowl.

2 **WASH** the coins in the dish soap to remove any dirt. Rinse and dry them off.

3 **USING THE SCISSORS,** cut the paper into four small squares, each just smaller than 1 inch (2.5 cm) on each side.

4 **PLACE** a penny on the strip of foil.

5 **SOAK** a paper square in the vinegar/salt solution. The square should be damp, but not dripping. Place the wet square on top of the penny.

6 **PLACE** a nickel on top of the paper.

7 **PLACE** a penny on top of the nickel.

8 **PLACE** another damp paper square on top of the penny.

9 **REPEAT** steps 6–8 until you end with a nickel on top.

10 **TOUCH** one end of the LED to the aluminum foil at the bottom of the stack and the other end to the nickel at the top of the stack.

WHAT'S GOING ON?

The battery you built was made out of two different metals. The vinegar/salt solution acted as an electrolyte. When two different metals are connected by an electrolyte, a chemical reaction occurs at the surface of these metals which either releases or accepts electrons. When the battery stack is connected to the LED, an electric current is created.

THINK ABOUT IT

What if you continued the pattern and made the battery stack taller? What do you think this would do to your battery?

VOLTAGE

THE FIRST BATTERY WAS CREATED BY ALESSANDRO VOLTA IN 1800. This was called the Volta Battery. To make the Volta Battery, he made a giant stack of alternating layers of zinc, blotting paper soaked in salt water, and silver. This early design for a battery is often called a voltaic pile.

DIFFICULTY

MINIMUM PEOPLE

GRAB AN ADULT!

MAGNETIZE IT!

Most of us know that **MAGNETS** have a way of "sticking" to metal objects. But why is that?

A magnet has two ends: a north pole and a south pole. The north pole of one magnet attracts the south pole of another magnet. But the north poles of two magnets will always repel each other. The south poles of two magnets will also always repel each other. A magnet has a force that flows from its north pole to its south pole. This force creates a magnetic field around the magnet, which attracts certain metals. Try it for yourself!

WHAT YOU'LL NEED

- 3 feet (0.9 m) of thinly coated copper wire

- Large metal nail

- New C or D battery

- Several metal, uncoated paper clips or other small metal objects

- Scissors, wire cutter, or coarse sandpaper

WHAT TO DO

1 WRAP the wire tightly around the nail. Leave 4 to 6 inches (10 to 15 cm) of wire extending from each end.

2 HAVE AN ADULT USE the scissors, wire cutter, or sandpaper to carefully shave about 1 inch (2.5 cm) of coating from each end of the wire until the copper underneath the coating is exposed. Be careful not to cut the wire under the coating. You just want to expose it from under its covering but not damage it.

3 SPREAD the paper clips out near your work area.

4 PRESS one end of the wire to the - side of the battery and the other end to the + side.

5 MOVE the nail near the paper clips and watch what happens.

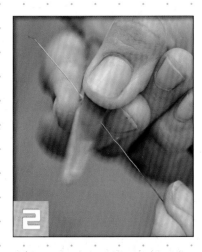
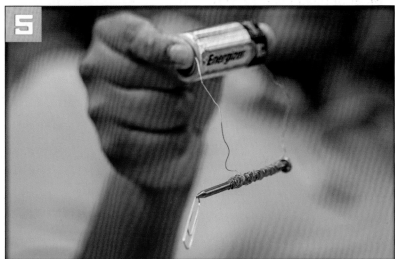

WHAT'S GOING ON?

The battery produces an electrical current that flows through the copper wire. This creates a magnetic field around the wire, magnetizing the metal of the nail. When you disconnect the wire from the battery, the circuit breaks and the magnetic field stops.

THINK ABOUT IT

Do you think your electromagnet would work if the copper coils were not wound as tightly around the nail?

CHARGED-UP EARTH

EARTH IS ACTUALLY A GIANT MAGNET.
This is because the planet's center is a metal core made of iron, which behaves like a magnet. Just like any magnet, one end is the north pole and the other end is the south pole. This is why we have the names North Pole and South Pole for the opposite ends of Earth.

Our planet's giant magnetic field is what allows magnetic compasses to work. You probably know that a compass needle always points north. This is because the needle is a magnet. The north pole of one magnet is always attracted to the south pole of another magnet. In the case of the compass, the south pole of its magnetic needle points to the north pole of Earth's magnetic field.

SUN STOVE

DIFFICULTY

MINIMUM PEOPLE

GRAB AN ADULT!

The sun has been producing energy for billions of years and is Earth's most important energy source. Energy that comes from the sun is called **SOLAR ENERGY.** Humans have used solar energy for centuries to heat their homes, cook their food, and even generate electricity.

Solar energy is a form of renewable energy: Unlike nonrenewable sources of energy, such as coal or oil, solar energy can never run out, no matter how much of it we consume. Plus, solar energy is considered "clean energy." That means that when we use solar energy, we're not polluting the environment. These qualities make solar energy extremely useful and important.

To top it off, solar energy can also be converted into heat energy. If you've ever sat in a car that's been parked in a sunny parking lot all day, you know what we mean. Ouch! See for yourself how solar energy works!

WHAT YOU'LL NEED

- Cardboard pizza box, cleaned
- Pencil, pen, or marker
- Ruler
- Scissors
- Aluminum foil
- Tape
- Several sheets of black construction paper
- Plastic wrap
- Newspapers
- S'mores ingredients: chocolate, marshmallows, and graham crackers
- A sunny day

CONTINUE TO NEXT PAGE

NOTE! Solar ovens are most effective between the hours of 11 a.m. and 2 p.m., when the sun's rays are strongest.

WHAT TO DO

1 PLACE a sheet of construction paper horizontally in the center of the top flap of the pizza box. Trace the outline of the paper.

2 USE the scissors to carefully cut along three of the four sides of the rectangle you drew on the top. Do not cut along the fourth edge. Instead, fold the rectangle back along this edge, so that it acts like a flap.

3 CUT a piece of aluminum foil the size of the flap you made in the previous step. Tape the aluminum foil to the underside of the flap.

4 CUT two pieces of plastic wrap the same size as the flap opening. Stretch one piece of plastic wrap tightly along the underside of the opening you made and tape it securely in place. Tape the second piece of plastic wrap to the outside of the opening.

5 LINE the bottom of the pizza box with several sheets of black construction paper. Use the tape to secure the papers in place.

6 ROLL several pieces of newspaper into tubes and stuff them into the sides of the box, making sure you can still close the lid of the box.

7 ARRANGE your s'mores ingredients on the black construction paper. Put a few pieces of chocolate on top of the graham crackers. Set one or two marshmallows on top of the chocolate.

8 PLACE the paper "dish" in the pizza box. Prop the flap open and face the box so the opening is in the direction of the sun.

9 WHEN THE S'MORES ARE READY, carefully remove them from the solar oven. Careful! The oven and the s'mores are hot. It's a good idea to ask an adult for help.

7

WHAT'S GOING ON?

There are several things working together to help convert the sun's energy into heat. The flap was covered with aluminum foil, which directs the sun's energy into the oven. The black paper lining the bottom of the oven absorbs the sun's energy and helps heat the oven. The plastic wrap used to seal the opening in the top of the box keeps the heat trapped in the oven. The newspapers lining the oven were used to insulate the oven and prevent heat from escaping through the cardboard.

THINK ABOUT IT

What would happen if you lined the oven with white paper instead of black paper? Do you think it's helpful to have the chocolate on top of the marshmallows instead of the marshmallows on top of the chocolate? Which would absorb more energy? What foods can you make in your solar oven?

9

SUN-CHARGED!

THE ENERGY SOURCES WE HAVE BECOME DEPENDENT ON, LIKE OIL AND COAL, ARE DWINDLING.
They are of limited supply, and once they are gone, they are probably gone for good. That's why it's so important to find alternative, renewable energy sources. The sun provides a steady supply of energy and is not in danger of running out. Harnessing the sun's energy and converting it to power and electricity is an excellent energy option.

A solar cell is an electric device that is able to trap sunlight and convert it into electricity. Solar cells are very small and are only able to trap a very small amount of solar energy. But by combining many solar cells together into a solar panel, it is possible to capture a lot of solar energy—enough to power a home.

Solar energy is an important, growing technology, but it's not perfect. Solar technologies are still being developed. The solar panels required to capture the solar energy are expensive. They also require a lot of space.

DIFFICULTY

MINIMUM PEOPLE

GRAB AN ADULT!

SOLAR UPDRAFT TOWER

When air is heated it expands, and when it expands it rises. This movement of air is called an **UPDRAFT.**

When warm air rises up a tower, it is called the chimney effect. You can see the chimney effect at work when you use a fireplace. As the fire heats the air around it, the warm air is forced up the chimney. As the hot air rises up the chimney, more hot air from the fire is pulled up after it. The result is a steady flow of hot air, otherwise called a draft, up the chimney.

Solar updraft towers use the chimney effect to produce energy. Since hot air rises, it's possible to take the energy of the moving air and convert it to usable energy. Try it for yourself!

WHAT YOU'LL NEED

- 3 aluminum cans, emptied and cleaned. Ask an adult to help you remove the bottoms and tops of the cans with a can opener.

- Masking tape or duct tape

- 1 paper clip

- 1 pushpin

- 1 6-inch (15-cm) square sheet of white paper

- 2 thick blocks or pieces of wood of the same thickness. If you don't have blocks available, thick books work as well.

- Indoor space with bright, direct sunlight

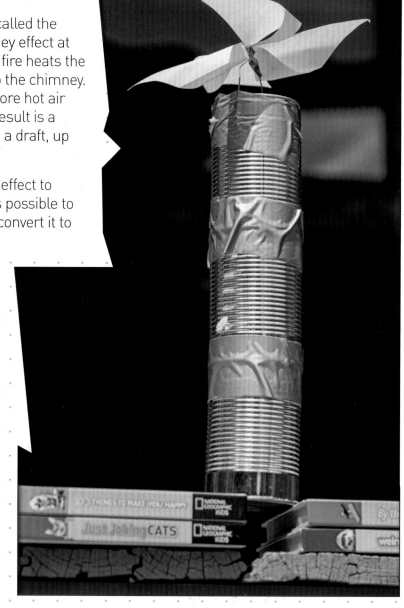

WHAT TO DO

1 STACK the three cans on top of each other and secure them together with the tape.

2 UNBEND the paper clip and form it into an arch shape.

3 USING THE TAPE, secure the arched paper clip across the top of the can tower.

4 USE the tape to carefully secure the pushpin to the center of the arch, with the pointy end facing up.

5 NEXT, you'll make a pinwheel from your sheet of paper. Cut diagonally from each of the four corners of the paper to about ¼ inch (0.6 cm) from the center.

6 BEND every other point from the corner to the center.

7 TAPE the points of the folded pieces to the center of the paper. Now you have your pinwheel!

8 CAREFULLY PIERCE the pinwheel's center with the pushpin.

9 PLACE the two blocks in front of a sunny window.

10 PLACE the tower on top of the two blocks, ensuring an air gap on the bottom of the tower.

11 WAIT for the sun to heat the area and watch the pinwheel spin.

WHAT'S GOING ON?

As the sun warms the air at the base of the column, that air becomes warmer than the air above it. Since the air is trapped in the tower, it's forced to rise up through the tower as it's warmed. As the warm air rises up the tower, the draft it creates pulls additional air up along with it. As the air stream gets drawn up the tower it pushes against the pinwheel's fins, causing it to spin just like a windmill.

💡 THINK ABOUT IT

How do you think your solar updraft tower would work if you made the tower taller by using four cans instead of three cans? Do you think your tower would work if you didn't place it on top of blocks? Why or why not?

> SOLVE THIS!
> ENERGY

We can thank energy for everything on Earth, from plants to our warm homes. Take a look at these scenarios, then grab your makerbox. Can you tinker up some solutions that put energy to use? Remember, there's no right answer!

SITUATION #1

You're a conservationist and you've been asked to assist with a recycling program at the landfill.

The city is looking to separate metal from landfill garbage. This metal could be reused to make new products, preventing waste. The landfill contains several acres of trash. It would take landfill workers an impossible amount of time to pick through the landfill in search of metal pieces. How can you quickly separate the metals from the trash?

SITUATION #2

As a community planner, you've noticed several abandoned lots in a neighborhood.

After talking with the community, many people have said they'd like to use the lots as community gardens. Can you design a program to clean up the lots and reuse some of the "trash" to make greenhouses for growing plants all year long?

SITUATION #3

You're designing a visitor center at a national park in a desert sanctuary.

The goal of your project is to create a sustainable, energy-efficient building that takes advantage of the area's natural features for heating and cooling. Your biggest concern, given the hot desert climate, is to design a building that doesn't get too hot and doesn't use too much air conditioning. How can you use the natural desert environment to design a sustainable building?

SITUATION #4

To study a kind of fish called koi, you've built a small pond.

When the upcoming weather forecast projects freezing temperatures, you begin to worry. While a little bit of ice is not dangerous for koi, if your pond freezes over the koi will not survive. How can you prevent your pond from freezing and keep the koi fish safe?

CHAPTER 6

ACOUSTICS

QUICK FACTS

Gently put your hand on your throat and hum your favorite song. What do you feel? Vibrations! **VIBRATIONS ALLOW US TO HEAR SOUNDS.** Here's how it works.

SOUND ENERGY

SOUND IS A TYPE OF ENERGY CAUSED BY VIBRATIONS. THESE VIBRATIONS BEGIN BECAUSE OF SOME KIND OF ACTION.

Take, for example, your hand knocking on a door. Your hand exerts a force on the door, causing a vibration of the molecules near the door. When those molecules vibrate, they in turn cause other molecules near them to vibrate, and so on and so on. As the vibration spreads from molecule to molecule, it becomes a sound wave. This sound wave eventually reaches your ear.

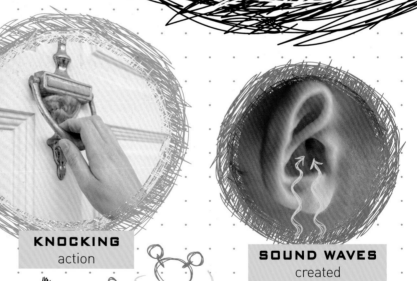

KNOCKING
action

MOLECULES
vibrate

SOUND WAVES
created

SOUND WAVES

SOUND WAVES CREATED BY VIBRATING MOLECULES MUST TRAVEL THROUGH MATTER—LIKE AIR, WATER, OR METAL.

Without matter, vibrations cannot spread from molecule to molecule. (That's why there's no sound in outer space. Since there is no atmosphere in space, there's no matter for the sound waves to move through.) Sound travels at different speeds depending on the type of matter it is traveling through. A sound in water travels faster than that same sound moving through air.

Some sounds are nice, like the sound of rain against a window, a baby giggling, or your favorite tune. Other sounds, like the noise of a blaring alarm or nails on a chalkboard, are not as pleasant.

LET'S EXPLORE WITH DIFFERENT SOUNDS AND VIBRATIONS.

GRAB AN ADULT!

STRING PHONE

Before everyone had cell phones, all **TELEPHONES** were connected by wires that carried the sound of one person's voice across some distance to another person's ear at the other end of the line. You can make your own telephone to see how the sound vibrations of your voice get carried along a wire. Try it for yourself!

WHAT YOU'LL NEED

- 2 large plastic cups
- Pushpin
- About 10 to 30 feet (3 to 10 m) of string
- 2 paper clips
- A friend

WHAT TO DO

1   USING THE PUSHPIN, poke a small hole into the bottom of both cups. Wiggle the pushpin around to make each hole big enough for the string to go through it. Ask an adult to help you with this step.

2   INSERT one end of the string into a cup through the bottom hole. Tie that end to a paper clip, so that when you pull the string tight, the paper clip rests against the inside bottom of the cup.

3   REPEAT this step with the other end of the string and your second cup.

4   GIVE one cup to your friend and keep the other cup for yourself. Walk slowly apart until the string connecting the two cups is straight and tight.

5   PUT your cup over your ear. Have your friend talk into their cup using a quiet voice. Can you hear your friend talking?

6   NOW SWITCH. You talk quietly into your cup and have your friend listen. Can your friend hear you?

7   NOW LET the string go slack and try having a conversation with your friend. Can you still hear each other?

Landline phones work much the same way as your string phone. But with landline phones, your voice's sound waves are converted into electricity, which can travel farther.

WHAT'S GOING ON?

When you talked into the cup, your voice made the air inside the cup vibrate. This made the bottom of the cup vibrate, which then made the paper clip and the string vibrate. The vibrations continued to travel across the string, through your friend's cup, and finally reached your friend's ear as sound. For the sound to travel along this path, the string must be kept taut. When the string goes slack, the vibrations don't have a solid path to travel through and begin to lose their energy, eventually fading before reaching your friend's ear.

THINK ABOUT IT

Since the speed of sound is affected by the type of matter it moves through, how would your phone work if you replaced the string with yarn, fishing wire, or cotton fabric? You might want to try it!

GRAB AN ADULT!

SILLY NOISEMAKER

Whether you're listening to a rock concert or a whisper, everything you hear is created by sound waves. So why are some sounds so quiet and others super loud? It's all about energy.

Imagine you gently pluck a string on a guitar. The vibrations you created produce a sound. Now pluck that same string more forcefully. The note doesn't change, but the volume increases. The sound is louder because you transferred more energy to the string. Because it received more energy, the string vibrated more. **AMPLITUDE** is a word used to describe the intensity of the vibrations. The higher the amplitude, the louder the sound. Try it for yourself!

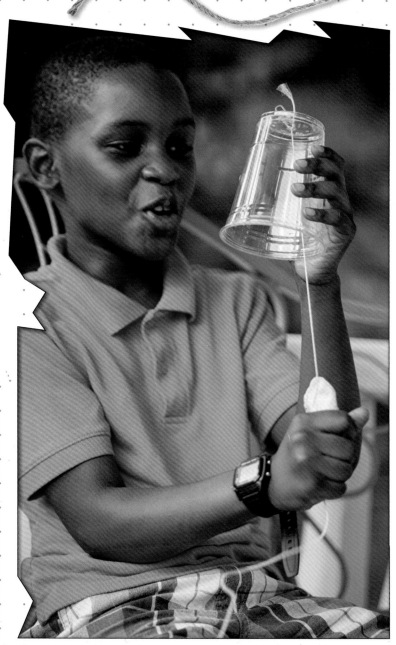

WHAT YOU'LL NEED

- Plastic cup
- Pushpin
- About 16 to 20 inches (40 to 50 cm) of string
- Paper clip
- Paper towel
- Water

WHAT TO DO

1   USING THE PUSHPIN, poke a small hole into the bottom of the cup. Wiggle the pushpin around to make the hole big enough for the string to go through it. Ask an adult to help you with this step.

2   INSERT one end of the string into the hole through the bottom of the cup.

3   TIE a paper clip to the end remaining outside the cup, so that when you pull the string tight, the paper clip rests against the outside of the cup.

4   FOLD a small square of paper towel and moisten it slightly with water. The paper towel should be damp but not dripping wet.

5   HOLDING THE CUP upside down, so the open end of the cup is facing downward, wrap the damp paper towel around the string and pull it down.

WHAT'S GOING ON?

When you pull on the string, you cause it to vibrate. If the string were not attached to the cup, the vibrations along the string would be almost silent. But because the string is attached to the cup, the vibrations travel up the string and into the cup where the vibrations are amplified, or made louder. The louder sound is produced because the sound wave from the string spreads to the cup, which has a much larger surface area than the string. The larger surface area allows for a louder sound.

THINK ABOUT IT

Why do you use a wet paper towel for this activity? Do you think you'd get the same or different results with a dry paper towel? Try it!

SHHHHHHHHHH!

THE INTENSITY OF A SOUND IS MEASURED IN DECIBELS, WHICH IS ABBREVIATED AS dB.

A whisper is in the range of 15 dB, while a normal conversation is about 60 dB. A DJ dance party is around 110 dB. As you get farther away from the source of the sound, the decibel level, as it is perceived by you, drops. The sound of the dance party is still at the same intensity, but it becomes quieter to your ears as you walk away from the area.

Any sound above 85 dB can harm your hearing if your ears are exposed to that intensity often and for long stretches of time. You know you are listening to a sound over 85 dB if you have to raise your voice to be heard. Over time, repeated exposure to loud noises can affect your hearing. So lower the volume on your headphones! Your ears will thank you.

DIFFICULTY

MINIMUM PEOPLE

SOUND WAVE STETHOSCOPE

AMPLIFICATION of sound helps us hear more clearly. Sometimes sound waves are amplified by electricity, such as in an amplifier you can buy at the store or one attached to a microphone. Other times, sound waves are amplified by simply helping the vibrations reach your ear more directly. You know that sound waves need to travel through a medium to your ears. Usually, when sound waves are traveling through the air, they can travel outward in different directions. Only some of the waves make it to your ears. To help direct more of the sound waves to your ears, you can give them a specific path to travel through. Try it for yourself!

WHAT YOU'LL NEED

- About 4 feet (1.2 m) of string or yarn

- Metal spoon

- Wooden ruler

- Scissors

- A friend

WHAT TO DO

1 **BEGIN** a knot in the middle of the string, but don't pull it tight—you'll want to have an open loop. Insert the handle of the spoon through the loop and pull tightly so the string is tied securely to the spoon. You should have two long pieces of string of approximately equal lengths dangling from the spoon.

2 **TAKE** both ends of the string and wrap one around the pointer finger of your hand. Do the same with the other end and your other hand.

3 **PUSH** the string against the inside of your ears. Be sure not to stick your fingers into your ears, just rest them against the inner part of your ear.

4 **LET** the spoon hang down so it's not resting against your body. You may need to lean your head forward a bit.

5 **HAVE** your friend hit the ruler against the round part of the spoon.

WHAT'S GOING ON?

When the ruler hits the spoon, it causes the metal in the spoon to vibrate. The vibrations then travel up the string and into your ears.

THINK ABOUT IT

Would the length of the string affect the sound that reaches your ear? What if you used a plastic spoon instead of a metal spoon?

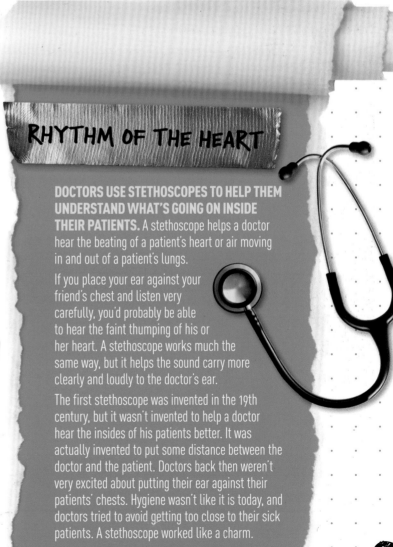

RHYTHM OF THE HEART

DOCTORS USE STETHOSCOPES TO HELP THEM UNDERSTAND WHAT'S GOING ON INSIDE THEIR PATIENTS. A stethoscope helps a doctor hear the beating of a patient's heart or air moving in and out of a patient's lungs.

If you place your ear against your friend's chest and listen very carefully, you'd probably be able to hear the faint thumping of his or her heart. A stethoscope works much the same way, but it helps the sound carry more clearly and loudly to the doctor's ear.

The first stethoscope was invented in the 19th century, but it wasn't invented to help a doctor hear the insides of his patients better. It was actually invented to put some distance between the doctor and the patient. Doctors back then weren't very excited about putting their ear against their patients' chests. Hygiene wasn't like it is today, and doctors tried to avoid getting too close to their sick patients. A stethoscope worked like a charm.

KAZOO

You can't have music without sound, but not all sounds are music. In general, **MUSICAL SOUNDS** are somewhat ordered, meaning the sound waves usually come in recognizable patterns. Nonmusical sounds are called noise. Noise is made up of mostly irregular or disordered groupings of sound waves.

But it's not always so simple. One person's noise might be another person's music, or vice versa. What matters is that you like what you're listening to. So get out there, get creative, and make some sweet sounds with an instrument of your very own.

WHAT YOU'LL NEED

- Empty paper towel tube
- Scissors
- Wax paper
- Rubber band
- Sharpened pencil

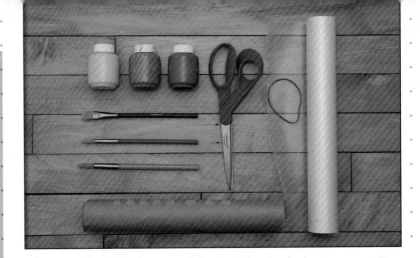

WHAT TO DO

1 USING THE SCISSORS, cut out a square of wax paper slightly bigger than the width of the paper towel tube opening.

2 COVER one end of the paper towel tube with the wax paper square and secure it in place, tightly, with the rubber band.

3 USING THE SHARPENED PENCIL, carefully poke four holes down a line through the paper towel tube. It doesn't matter exactly where the holes are.

4 PLACE the open end of the kazoo up to your mouth and hum into the tube. You can also try saying "do" or "woo" over and over again into the kazoo to try making different sounds. Try covering and uncovering the holes as you hum.

Real kazoos also use a flimsy membrane—much like wax paper. The membrane can be found in the center tower of the instrument.

2

JOIN THE BAND

MUSICIANS PLAY WOODWIND INSTRUMENTS BY BLOWING AIR ACROSS OR INTO A MOUTHPIECE (HENCE THE "WIND" IN "WOODWIND") and using their fingers to open or close holes along the top to change the pitch (how high or low the sound is). A flute player, for example, holds the instrument sideways and blows air across the mouthpiece. A recorder player holds it upright and blows air into the mouthpiece. In both cases, the air travels down the instrument and causes vibrations to produce sound.

Like woodwinds, brass instruments, such as the trumpet and trombone, require air to make sound. But rather than blowing air, brass musicians vibrate their lips by buzzing them against a cup-shaped mouthpiece.

WHAT'S GOING ON?

As you hum into the kazoo, the sound waves of your voice travel down the paper towel tube. Some of the waves hit the wall of the paper towel tube, bouncing off of it. Some of the waves escape through the open holes. The rest of the sound hits the wax paper, causing the wax paper to vibrate. Since the wax paper is light and thin, it vibrates very quickly, changing the sound of your voice.

💡 THINK ABOUT IT

What if you used a different material to cover the end of your kazoo, like paper, aluminum foil, or cloth? Would this change the sound produced? Try it for yourself!

DIFFICULTY

MINIMUM PEOPLE

GUITAR

The guitar is one of the most popular instruments around the world, and different cultures have different variations of the instruments. Russians use a version of the guitar called the balalaika. Indian cultures have a version called the sitar, and Polynesia uses a ukulele. But even though the designs for all these guitars are somewhat different, they all make music the same way: by plucking or strumming strings, which creates sound vibrations. Try it for yourself!

WHAT YOU'LL NEED

- Empty rectangular tissue box or shoebox

- Scissors

- Empty paper towel tube

- Permanent marker

- 4 rubber bands, preferably in different widths

- Clear tape

WHAT TO DO

1   IF THE TISSUE BOX opening still has plastic around the edges, remove the plastic using the scissors. (If you don't have a tissue box, you can just cut a hole in the top of a shoebox.)

2   HOLD the box so that the hole faces you and stand it up on the narrow end of the box. Place the paper towel tube on top of the box, so that it stands vertically.

3   TRACE the base of the paper towel tube with your marker. Put the paper towel tube to the side for now, and use scissors to cut along the traced line. This will make a circle cutout.

4   INSERT the paper towel tube in the hole in the side of the tissue box. Use the tape to secure it tightly in place.

5   WRAP four rubber bands around the box the long way, making sure they cover the hole on the front of the box. Use rubber bands of different widths to create different tones and sounds.

6   STRUM the guitar like a rock star!

WHAT'S GOING ON?

When you pluck a rubber band on the guitar, you cause it to vibrate. The vibration travels through the rubber band and across the surface of the box and into the hole. The open area inside the box increases the amount of matter that is vibrating, causing the sound to be amplified.

THINK ABOUT IT

Try plucking a rubber band held between your fingers. How loud is the sound of the rubber band suspended in air compared to the rubber bands attached to the box?

DIFFICULTY

MINIMUM PEOPLE

DRUMS

Hit, shake, or scrape a **PERCUSSION INSTRUMENT,** and you'll hear its signature sound. Think of large drums like timpani, rattly maracas, and crashing cymbals. Each instrument produces only a few notes, depending on how and where they're struck. Their music is created by varying the rhythms and the beat. Try it for yourself!

WHAT YOU'LL NEED

- Empty aluminum can or plastic jug, cleaned

- Balloon

- Scissors

- Rubber band

- 2 unsharpened pencils

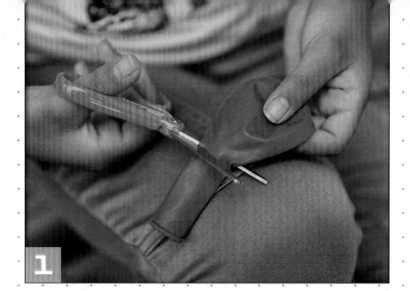

1

WHAT TO DO

1 USING THE SCISSORS, cut the narrow neck off the balloon so only the round part of the balloon remains.

2 CAREFULLY STRETCH the balloon across the opening of the tin can or jug. Use the rubber band to secure it tightly in place. This is the top of your drum.

3 USE the pencils as drumsticks and tap the top of the drum.

2

WHAT'S GOING ON?

When the pencil strikes the top of the drum, it causes the balloon to vibrate. Beneath the balloon, in the tin can or jug, is an open space, which amplifies the sound of the vibrations. The loudness of the sound produced depends on how forcefully you strike the drum. If you hit the drum hard, you will transfer more energy and produce a louder sound.

HEARING HOUND

YOU MAY HAVE WONDERED WHY YOUR DOG BARKS AT THE DOOR WHEN YOU DON'T HEAR ANYTHING, only to have someone knock on your door a moment later. How did your pup know? He heard! Dogs have much better hearing than humans. Their ears have up to 18 muscles, while human ears have only six. This allows dogs to move their ears to help funnel sound into their inner ear. Can you move your ears? You might be able to wiggle them, but your pup can tilt, turn, and raise his!

Dogs can also hear sounds that humans cannot. Human ears can hear sounds in a narrow frequency band, but dog ears can hear a much wider range of frequencies. That's why a dog whistle may be silent to our ears, but not to your dog's.

THINK ABOUT IT

What if the balloon across the top of the can was stretched more or less tightly? How would this affect the sound of the drum? Try it for yourself!

DIFFICULTY

MINIMUM PEOPLE

XYLOPHONE

Like a drum, a xylophone is played by striking the instrument with a stick or mallet. But there is one big difference between a drum and a xylophone: A xylophone is like a bunch of smaller percussion instruments in one. Each part of the xylophone plays a different note. When played with two mallets, you can make chords. Try it for yourself!

WHAT YOU'LL NEED

- 5 identical mason jars or glass bottles with lids

- Water

- Food coloring in assorted colors

- Wooden pencil

WHAT TO DO

1   ARRANGE the jars in a straight line on a flat table.

2   FILL the first jar with water almost to the top. Fill the next jar with slightly less water. Continue filling each of the jars down the line with water so that each jar has less water than the jar before it. Do not cap the jars.

3   PUT a few drops of food coloring in each of the bottles so that each is a different color. Then put the tops on the jars.

4   GENTLY TAP the pencil against the tops or sides of the jars. How is the sound of each different?

WHAT'S GOING ON?

When you tap the glass, the vibrations in the glass pass into the water. The amount of water in each glass affects the sound that is produced. The deepest sound comes from striking the container with the greatest amount of water. This is because the water makes the glass heavier, so it is harder for the glass walls to vibrate. Thus the sound wave generated by the vibrations is slower, or has a lower frequency. The frequency of sound waves determines the pitch—that is, how high or low a sound is. So, the more water there is in the jar, the lower the frequency and the lower or deeper the sound.

THINK ABOUT IT

Would the sound change if you used a metal spoon instead of a wooden pencil to tap the glass? What if you replaced the water with milk or juice? Do you think this will affect the sound?

Sound waves not only bring you your favorite tunes, they're helpful, too. Take a look at these scenarios, then grab your makerbox. Can you tinker up some sound-based solutions? Remember, there's no right answer!

SITUATION #1

You're a cartographer mapping Australia's Great Barrier Reef.

You want to know whether the reef is growing or shrinking each year. You know that submarines use a system called sonar to detect objects in the water. Sonar works by sending out sound pulses, then measuring how long it takes for the sound to reflect back. Can you think of a way to use sonar to track how the Great Barrier Reef changes?

You're on assignment in a rural village.

You're inspecting the village well and wondering how deep into the ground it descends. Trying to look down into the dark opening doesn't help. You cannot make out the bottom. You grab a nearby stone off the ground and decide to drop it down the well. Eventually it will need to hit bottom. The well can't go on forever. Can you think of a way to use the sound of the stone hitting bottom to calculate the depth of the well?

SITUATION #2

SITUATION #3

You're a biologist studying howler monkeys in the rain forests of Central America.

Lucky for you, howler monkeys are one of the loudest animals in the rain forest, so finding them shouldn't be too difficult. Their voices are so loud, they can be heard from miles away. There's just one problem. Here in the rain forest there are plenty of competing sounds from every direction. Can you think of a way to filter the sounds of the howler monkeys to determine a more precise location for their troop?

SITUATION #4

As a park ranger, you're concerned about noise pollution in protected areas.

You know that, just like air pollution, noise pollution could have a negative impact on the ecosystem. Noises that aren't naturally occurring, like airplanes flying overhead, cars driving on nearby highways, or campers setting up campsites, could frighten, distract, and harm the animals. Can you design a solution to reduce the level of noise pollution in the park?

CHAPTER 7

FORCES

QUICK FACTS

You can't see them, and you might not even notice them, but **THERE ARE FORCES ALL AROUND YOU—ALL THE TIME!** Are you sitting in a chair reading this? The chair is exerting a force against you. Are you outside? Every time you feel a breeze, the wind is exerting a force, too.

Forces make a ball fall to the ground, a sailboat glide across the sea, a car increase its speed, or a magnet attract a piece of metal. Forces are even at work in outer space, creating the movement of the planets around the sun— and a whole lot more.

Let's take a look at some forces at work.
Imagine a soccer ball laying still on the ground.

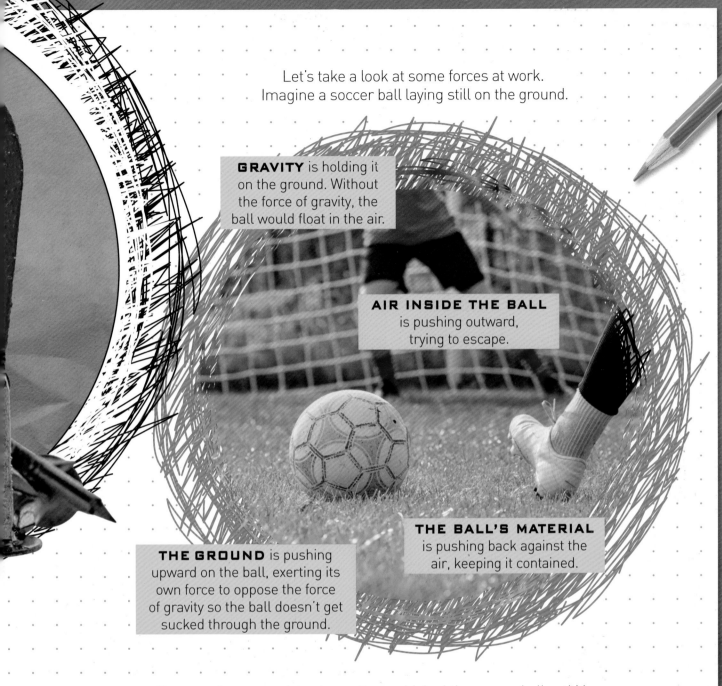

GRAVITY is holding it on the ground. Without the force of gravity, the ball would float in the air.

AIR INSIDE THE BALL is pushing outward, trying to escape.

THE BALL'S MATERIAL is pushing back against the air, keeping it contained.

THE GROUND is pushing upward on the ball, exerting its own force to oppose the force of gravity so the ball doesn't get sucked through the ground.

So many forces, and you haven't even kicked the soccer ball yet! Now go ahead and kick it. Your foot exerts a force of energy against the ball, sending it soaring in the air. If you kick the ball very hard, exerting a lot of force, the ball will travel far. But there are forces acting against the ball as it travels through the air, slowing it down, and, eventually, making the ball stop.

LET'S EXPLORE SOME DIFFERENT FORCES.

DIFFICULTY

MINIMUM PEOPLE

WATER BALLOON HELMET

When you drop something, it falls to the ground. When you jump up, you come back down. Everything that goes up (on Earth) must come down because of the force of **GRAVITY.**

When an object falls, gravity pulling down on the object causes it to pick up speed as it travels.

The speed an object is traveling affects the force with which the object hits the ground—the faster the speed, the greater the force. So, because objects increase in speed as they fall, the greater the height an object falls from, the greater the force when it hits the ground.

Your mission: Make a helmet for a water balloon so it doesn't break when dropped to the ground from different heights.

WHAT YOU'LL NEED

- Water balloon filled with water

- Permanent marker

- Other materials to build a helmet for your water balloon. You might use paper towel tubes, cotton balls, cloth, tissues, newspaper, bubble wrap, drinking straws, egg cartons, masking tape—whatever!

WHAT TO DO

1 DRAW a face on your water balloon with the marker. It can be silly, serious, or anything you like. Have fun with it!

2 CHOOSE a spot outside where you'll be testing your helmet. It should be a spot that can withstand getting wet.

3 USE the materials you've gathered to design a helmet for the balloon. Just like a bike helmet doesn't cover your face, make sure the water balloon's "face" isn't covered by the helmet you design. The water balloon should still be able to "see"!

4 THINK about how you might protect the water balloon from breaking upon impact. How can you soften the blow so the balloon stays intact? Will your helmet protect the balloon from the height of the drop in your selected spot?

5 NOW TEST your helmet! Go to your selected spot and try dropping the balloon with its helmet from a lower height. Did the balloon survive? If so, try again with a different balloon and new helmet design. If it survived, keep raising the start height until it finally pops.

WHAT'S GOING ON?

When the water balloon hits the ground, the force of the impact with the ground pushes against the balloon, causing it to come to a complete stop. Just like a helmet you use when riding a bike, the cushioning layer of the balloon's helmet softens the blow because it reduces the force applied to the balloon from its impact with the ground. A well-designed helmet will also distribute the force around the helmet so that less of the total force is applied against one impact point.

THINK ABOUT IT
How much higher was the breaking point's start height than your first height? How could you modify your helmet to protect the balloon from that height?

HARD HEAD

THE BRAIN IS RESPONSIBLE FOR ALL OF THE BODY'S FUNCTIONS: IT KEEPS OUR HEART BEATING, OUR LUNGS BREATHING, AND ALLOWS US TO TALK, MOVE, LEARN, AND REMEMBER.

Since our brain is so important, maybe we should walk around in helmets to make sure our brain is protected. Well, we actually do.

Your skull is a built-in helmet that protects your soft, spongy brain. Thanks to 22 strong skull bones, three thin membranes called meninges, and a cushion of cerebrospinal fluid, small bumps don't damage that wrinkly organ that is your body's command center.

If you bump your head on a door frame or hit it slipping on a slick sidewalk, it may hurt, and you may even get a goose egg, but thanks to your skull, you'll probably be all right.

While your skull does protect against minor knocks and jolts, it's still important to use a helmet for high-speed activities like bicycling, skating, and skiing, where it's possible to fall fast and hard.

DIFFICULTY

MINIMUM PEOPLE

CATAPULT

Imagine you're a pitcher in a baseball game. You get into a windup position, ready to throw a killer pitch across the plate, and ... STOP! Just before you release the ball from your hand, it is bursting with **POTENTIAL ENERGY,** the energy that's stored inside an object just before it is set into motion.

Once the ball is in motion, the potential energy is converted into kinetic energy. You can think of potential energy as kinetic energy waiting to happen and kinetic energy as the energy of motion. The more potential energy stored in the ball, the more kinetic energy it will have. That means it will be able travel farther and faster.

The same concept applies to any object tossed, launched, or hurled from a state of rest into a state of motion. Try it for yourself!

WHAT YOU'LL NEED

- 7 wooden craft sticks

- 3 rubber bands

- A milk cap or bottle cap

- Glue

- Cotton balls or other lightweight objects to launch

1 STACK five of the craft sticks together and secure both ends of the stack with one rubber band on each side. Make sure each rubber band is tightly wrapped around the ends of the craft sticks so the craft sticks cannot slide apart.

2 STACK the remaining two craft sticks together. Secure one end of the sticks tightly with a rubber band.

3 TAKE the stack of two craft sticks and pull the sticks apart at the open end. Slide the stack of five craft sticks you made in step 1 between the two craft sticks as far down as they can comfortably go.

4 GLUE the milk cap to the topmost craft stick, so that the top of the cap is glued to the surface of the craft stick. Allow the glue to completely dry.

5 NOW it's time to launch! Place the cotton ball into the milk cap. Use the tip of your finger to push down on the milk cap, then release!

WHAT'S GOING ON?

When the catapult is at rest, before you push the cap down, it has no stored, or potential, energy. When you push down on the milk cap, you change the catapult from a state of rest and give the catapult potential energy. When you release the catapult, the stored potential energy is converted to kinetic energy, and the projectile goes flying!

THRILLER RIDE

IF YOU'VE EVER ENJOYED THE THRILL OF A ROLLER COASTER, YOU'VE EXPERIENCED THE BACK AND FORTH BETWEEN POTENTIAL AND KINETIC ENERGY.

Most roller coaster cars are pulled up the first hill by a chain. As the car climbs, it gains potential energy. At the very top of the first hill, the car has a lot of stored potential energy. The moment the car is released, the potential energy is converted into kinetic energy and you zoom down the coaster's drop. Then the car begins to climb the next hill, using some of its remaining kinetic energy to move up the hill. This swapping between potential and kinetic energy continues throughout the thrilling ride.

THINK ABOUT IT

Instead of pushing the craft stick all the way down, push it only halfway and then launch the projectile. How far did the projectile travel this time? Why do you think the projectile's travel path was different?

DIFFICULTY

MINIMUM PEOPLE

GRAB AN ADULT!

BALL LAUNCHER

Rubber bands are masters of harnessing the potential-to-kinetic-energy conversion power. When you stretch out a rubber band, you take it from its state of rest to being full of potential energy. In fact, this kind of potential energy is called **ELASTIC POTENTIAL ENERGY,** and it happens when something stretchy wants to return from a stretched-out position to its normal resting position. Try it for yourself!

WHAT YOU'LL NEED

- An empty plastic water bottle with its cap
- Ruler
- Scissors
- 2 rubber bands
- Thumbtack
- About 12 inches (30 cm) of string
- A large, round bead with a hole through the center
- Table-tennis ball

WHAT TO DO

1   USING THE RULER, measure approximately 4 inches (10.2 cm) down the side of the water bottle, starting from the bottom of the cap. Mark that spot on the side of the bottle. Rotate the bottle and repeat this step two more times, then draw a line around the bottle, connecting the three marks. Ask an adult to help you cut along this line to divide the water bottle into two pieces. Keep the part of the bottle that is connected to the cap. (You can save the bottom half and the cap in your makerbox for another project.)

2   USING THE SCISSORS, make four notches around the open water bottle edge. They should be evenly spaced from one another. Each notch should be approximately 0.5 inch (1.3 cm) deep.

3   INSERT the first rubber band through two notches opposite each other, then twist and stretch the rubber band around the outside of the bottle. Repeat this step with the other rubber band using the remaining two notches. The two rubber bands should now form an X shape across the opening of the bottle.

4   TIE OR LOOP the string at the point where the two rubber bands cross in the bottle opening. Then run the string through the neck of the bottle and out through the cap opening.

5   THREAD the string through the bead and tie a knot to fasten the bead to the string.

6   PLACE the table-tennis ball on the rubber bands. Pull back on the bead to stretch the rubber bands. Then release!

WHAT'S GOING ON?

When you pull back on the bead, the string pulls the rubber bands, moving them from their state of rest and stretching them. Stretched out, the rubber bands house potential energy. When you release the bead, the rubber bands snap back to their original state of rest. The energy transfers to the ball, making it fly.

TOWER CHALLENGE

Have you ever wondered why skyscrapers don't just fall over? The massive size and height of these towers appear to defy gravity. Yet engineers design them to be strong enough to withstand the various forces acting on them, such as gravity, torsion (a twisting force that wind can exert), and compression.

COMPRESSION—the pushing or squeezing of a material—comes from the weight of the building itself. Imagine the hundreds or thousands of bricks or pounds of cement used to build a tower. Now add other building materials, furniture, equipment, and the hundreds of people living or working inside. That's a lot of weight!

Clearly, engineers have a lot to consider and calculate when designing a stable tower. Think you're up for the challenge? Try it for yourself!

The Parthenon

Buildings today frequently use cylindrical columns for strength and support. But it was the ancient Greeks, nearly 2,500 years ago, who first realized they could use cylindrical columns to build impressive structures.

The Parthenon is a temple in Athens, Greece, built thousands of years ago to honor the Greek goddess Athena. It is one of ancient Greece's most impressive architectural accomplishments, and most of it still stands today. The building was made using 46 cylindrical columns to support the roof, 8 across the front and back, and 17 on each side.

Ancient Greek architecture, and the Parthenon, has inspired many buildings through time. Next time you're out and about, try to spot buildings that use cylindrical columns.

WHAT YOU'LL NEED

- 3 sheets of sturdy construction paper or poster board

- Tape

- Several books to test the strength of your towers

- A flat surface

WHAT TO DO

FOLD THE FIRST paper in half the tall way, then in half again the tall way. Unfold the paper and use the folds to form the paper into a tall square tower. Use the tape to keep it closed.

1 FOLD the second paper in thirds to form the shape of a tall triangular tower.

2 ROLL the third paper into the shape of a tall, round, cylinder. Use the tape to keep it closed.

3 STAND the rectangular tower up on a flat surface. Begin stacking books on top of the tower. How many books were you able to stack before the tower collapsed?

4 NEXT, test the strength of your triangular tower. How many books were you able to stack before the tower collapsed?

5 FINALLY, TEST the strength of your cylindrical tower. How many books was this tower able to hold?

WHAT'S GOING ON?

Cylinders are one of the strongest shapes for building towers. This is because the cylinder doesn't have any edges like rectangular or triangular towers. A tower is only as strong as its weakest point, and the weakest point in the rectangular and triangular towers is at its folds. The cylindrical tower doesn't have any folds, so it can spread the load evenly across its entire surface.

TOWERING MECHANICS

SKYSCRAPERS MAY LOOK UNIQUE, BUT THEY SHARE SOME COMMON ELEMENTS. Working to resist the many forces acting on them and to bear their tremendous weight, most skyscrapers have a concrete foundation that anchors the building deep into the earth, and a grid-shaped steel skeleton that is the central support structure.

DIFFICULTY

MINIMUM PEOPLE

ROMAN ARCH

Created by the ancient Romans in the first century A.D., the **ARCH** is an engineering marvel. How can this horseshoe-shaped structure withstand the strong downward forces acting on it? It's because of both its overall shape and the shape of its individual blocks.

Precisely cut, wedge-shaped blocks are used to construct an arch. Downward forces pushing from the top of the arch squeeze the blocks together, and the forces are distributed evenly along the arch's curve. At the same time, the ground pushes up against the curve.

The forces are so strong that arches can stand without any glue or other adhesive holding them together. Try it for yourself!

WHAT YOU'LL NEED

- An ice cube tray that forms rectangular cubes that narrow slightly

- Water

- Paper towel

- Food coloring (optional)

- A friend

1   IF USING FOOD COLORING, place a few drops of food coloring into a container of water.

2   POUR the water into the ice cube tray, completely filling each of the compartments.

3   PLACE the filled ice cube tray in the freezer until completely frozen.

4   COVER your work area with the bath towel. When the ice is fully frozen, remove nine ice cubes from the tray and place them on the towel. Put the remaining ice cubes back into the freezer. They'll only be used in case one of the nine ice cubes you've selected becomes damaged or melts before you've finished your arch.

5   IT'S TIME to get to work on building the arch! Set the first two pieces of ice on the towel, a few inches apart. This will be the base of the arch.

6   STACK the next two pieces of ice on top of the base pieces. This is a good time to ask your friend to help hold the pieces in place for you until the arch is fully formed.

7   CONTINUE setting pieces into the formation, one on each side, so the arch is symmetrical. Your friend can continue to hold the arch stable as you work.

8   WHEN YOU HAVE four ice pieces on each side, you're ready to set the keystone, or center stone, in place. This will be the last piece of the arch and will hold the structure together. Before setting the keystone in place, visually inspect the arch you've assembled thus far. Does it look like the keystone can comfortably fit into the open space at the top of the arch? If the space appears to be too small, you may need to rebuild your arch with the base pieces starting a bit farther apart. If the space seems a little too big, see if you can slide the arch together once the keystone is in place. If the angle isn't quite right and you think you can do better, start all over! It's okay! It's fun trying to race against the clock to build the arch before your ice melts.

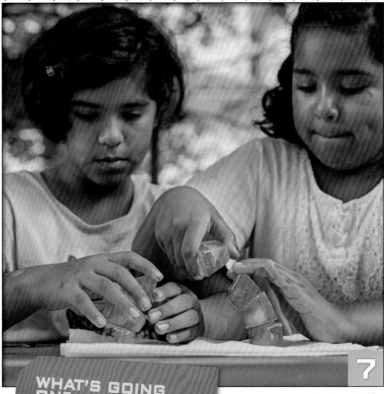

7

WHAT'S GOING ON?

The arch you built was constructed of blocks with a keystone in the center that held everything in place. The arch can stand upright without toppling over because of its unique shape. Downward forces from the top of the arch are spread out along the curve of the arch until the forces reach the base. At the same time, the ground pushes back with its own force. All of these forces act together to create a strong and sturdy structure.

Would your ice arch work if your ice pieces had a different shape?

DIFFICULTY

MINIMUM PEOPLE

TRUSS BRIDGE

Have you ever wondered how a bridge supports the weight of so many vehicles? Bridges need to withstand **COMPRESSION**—a squeezing force—and **TENSION**—a force that pulls materials apart. Bridges must also resist high wind conditions that create torsion, or twisting.

One shape resists these forces more than any other shape: the triangle. That's because it is able to distribute forces evenly across the span of a bridge and preserve its shape without bending. Try it for yourself!

WHAT YOU'LL NEED

- Approximately 70 craft sticks

- Wood glue

- Binder clips

- 1 Masking tape

WHAT TO DO

1 **LAY** one craft stick horizontally on your work surface and put a dab of glue on both ends. Take two more craft sticks. Place one stick on top of each dab of glue. Arrange the three sticks in a triangle shape.

2 **PUT** a dab of glue on the peak of the triangle connecting the three craft sticks together.

3 **PLACE** a dab of glue on the top peak of the triangle you just created, then secure another craft stick to it. Rotate the stick so it is horizontal.

13

4 PLACE a dab of glue on the end of the craft stick you just placed, then secure another craft stick from this point down to the first triangle you created. You should now have two attached triangles, one pointing up and the other pointing down.

5 CONTINUE with this pattern until you have seven triangles.

6 FASTEN binder clips to each connection point to help the glue dry in shape.

7 REPEAT steps 1 through 6 so you have two identical sides for your bridge. Set aside both side pieces until they are completely dry.

8 TO BUILD the bridge's base, begin by gluing four craft sticks together to form a square.

9 CONTINUE gluing squares to the first square you made, until you have four squares glued together in a line.

10 FASTEN binder clips to each connection point and set aside to dry.

11 WHEN THE THREE pieces you made are completely dry, remove the binder clips.

12 LAY the base across a flat surface. Take the two side pieces you constructed previously and hold them perpendicular (sideways) to the base, then angle the two side pieces toward each other so they form a triangle shape with the peak at the top.

13 USE the masking tape to secure the three pieces together, beginning at the top two corners then the bottom four corners. Then use the masking tape to secure the center of the bridge as needed.

14 TEST your bridge! Place your bridge across two chairs. Place the remaining craft sticks across your bridge's bottom. Place objects on the bottom crossbeams of your bridge.

4

11

WHAT'S GOING ON?

The bridge you built is called a truss bridge. The trusses are the connected triangular shapes that are able to support the forces placed on the bridge. These triangular trusses are strong because the forces acting upon the bridge are evenly distributed from the tops of the triangles down the base of each side of the triangle.

THINK ABOUT IT

What do you think is the weakest point on the bridge you built? Can you think of a way to make the truss bridge you built stronger so it can withstand even more weight?

DIFFICULTY

MINIMUM PEOPLE

GRAB AN ADULT!

FIDGET SPINNER

Forces don't only go up, down, and sideways. Sometimes, a force causes an object to move in circles. Think about the twisting motion you make when turning a bottle cap. That kind of force—one that causes rotational motion—is called **TORQUE.** To open the bottle, you need to keep applying torque to the cap until it is free. But sometimes, after an initial torque, an object that is moving along a circular path can continue spinning. The force that makes it continue to spin along a circular path is called **CENTRIPETAL FORCE.** Try it for yourself!

WHAT YOU'LL NEED

- Heavy cardboard, like the kind used for shipping packages
- Ruler
- Pencil
- Scissors
- Toothpicks
- 2 pennies
- Hot glue

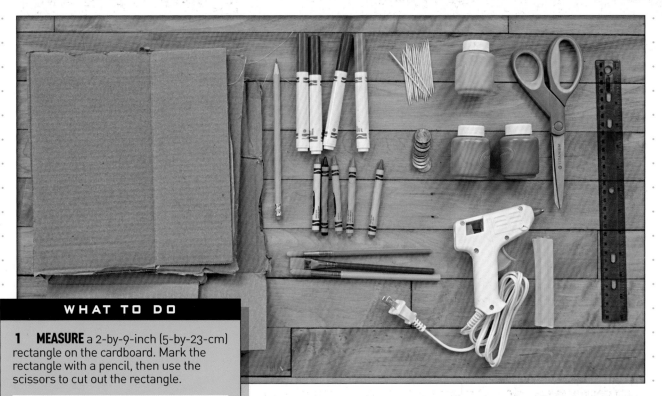

WHAT TO DO

1 **MEASURE** a 2-by-9-inch (5-by-23-cm) rectangle on the cardboard. Mark the rectangle with a pencil, then use the scissors to cut out the rectangle.

2 **USE** the ruler to draw a straight line from the top right corner of the rectangle to the bottom left corner of the rectangle. Then draw another straight line from the top left corner to the bottom right corner. You should now have an X drawn on the rectangle with the center of the X being at the middle of the cardboard rectangle.

3 **USE** the toothpick to poke a thin hole in the center of the X. Push the toothpick all the way through the cardboard, then remove the toothpick from the cardboard.

4 **TAKE** a penny and align its edge with the top, narrow side of the cardboard. Using the pencil, trace around the penny. Repeat this on the opposite narrow side of the cardboard. You should now have a circle outline on both ends of the cardboard. Using the scissors, cut out each circle, being careful not to cut farther into the cardboard rectangle than needed.

CONTINUE TO NEXT PAGE

WHAT TO DO (CONT'D)

5 **REPEAT** steps 1–4. You will now have two identical cardboard pieces and four cardboard circles.

6 **TAKE** a penny again and place it on the center of the X you drew on one cardboard rectangle. Slowly slide the penny out until the pencil lines of the X line up with the edges of the penny. Trace around the top side of the penny to create an arc between the lines of the X.

7 **REPEAT** step 6 with the other side of the X.

8 **DRAW** two lines to connect the two arcs, forming an oval. Cut out the oval. You can discard the rest of the cardboard rectangle or save it in your makerbox for other projects.

9 **REPEAT** steps 6–8 with the other cardboard rectangle.

10 **TAKE** the four cardboard circles you cut out and, using the toothpick, poke a hole through the center of one of the cardboard circles. Push the toothpick all the way through the cardboard, then remove the toothpick from the cardboard. Repeat this same process with the other three cardboard circles.

11 **TAKE** one of the oval cardboard pieces and lay it on a flat surface. Ask an adult to put a dab of hot glue on opposite ends of the oval, near the rounded edges. Place a penny on each dab of hot glue. Let it dry.

12 **INSERT** the toothpick through the center hole of one of the cardboard circles, then through the center hole of the oval with the pennies glues on, then through two more cardboard circles, then through the other oval, followed by the final cardboard circle. Leave space between each piece.

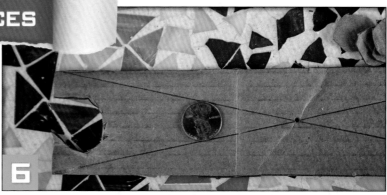

13 **ASK** an adult to place a dab of hot glue on top of each penny, then slide the second cardboard oval down. The pennies should now be glued to the ends of both pieces.

14 **WHEN IT IS DRY,** ask an adult to use the hot glue to glue around the top and bottom of the toothpick so it is secured to the outside cardboard circles.

15 **WHEN THE GLUE** is completely dry, use the scissors to cut away both ends of the toothpick poking out from the fidget spinner. The toothpick should be mostly even with the cardboard circles. You may want to ask an adult to use the hot glue again to cover the cut edges of the toothpick.

16 **WHEN ALL THE GLUE** is completely dry, it's time to spin! Hold the fidget spinner by pinching your thumb and forefinger on the outside cardboard circles. Use your other hand to spin the spinner!

Check out natgeokids.com /makethis to watch a step-by-step video of this activity.

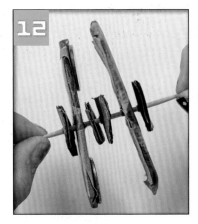

WHAT'S GOING ON?

When you flick the fidget spinner to start its motion, you are exerting a torque on the spinner. Once the fidget spinner is rotating, centripetal force keeps it spinning. Eventually, the fidget spinner stops because of the force of friction acting against the centripetal forces.

ROUND AND ROUND

YOU MIGHT SEE CENTRIPETAL FORCE AT WORK WHEN RIDING A ROLLER COASTER. Have you ever wondered why you don't fall out of the roller coaster, even when it whips you upside down through loops? Sure, seat belts and harnesses help keep you safe, but centripetal force also helps keeps you in your seat even when you're upside down in a loop. This is because once your body starts traveling in a circular motion, centripetal force takes over, causing your body to stay in circular motion. That's how you remain safely in your seat.

Pushes and pulls make everything happen! Take a look at these scenarios, then grab your makerbox. Can you tinker up some solutions that harness the power of forces? Remember, there's no right answer!

SITUATION #1

After several days of mountaineering, your clothes are starting to get pretty dirty.

You find a creek and decide it would be a good idea to rinse the grime from your socks. They're much cleaner now, but you realize you have no way to quickly dry them. You obviously don't have a clothes dryer to spin your socks dry in the mountains. Can you rig something to dry your sopping socks quickly so you can be on your way?

SITUATION #2

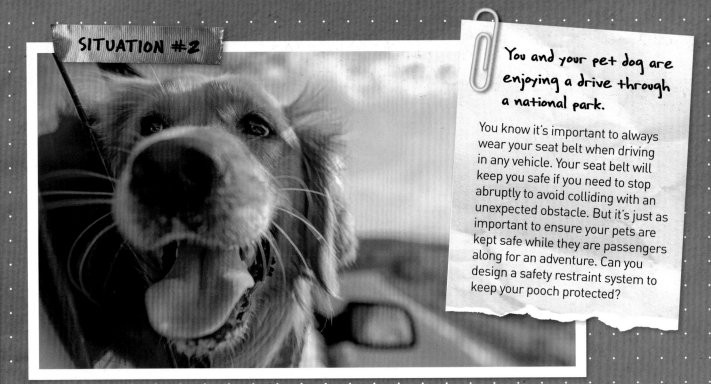

You and your pet dog are enjoying a drive through a national park.

You know it's important to always wear your seat belt when driving in any vehicle. Your seat belt will keep you safe if you need to stop abruptly to avoid colliding with an unexpected obstacle. But it's just as important to ensure your pets are kept safe while they are passengers along for an adventure. Can you design a safety restraint system to keep your pooch protected?

SITUATION #3

You're an environ-mentalist studying soil along coastal villages.

It's important to understand the composition of the soil because this information helps the villages know how to reduce the effects of erosion on their land. The soil in this region contains minerals, organic matter, and water. To study the makeup of the soil you'll need to find a way to isolate these soil components. How might you go about separating and isolating the components of the soil?

SITUATION #4

You're visiting the Costa Rican rain forest.

To get a panoramic view of this remarkable ecosystem, you've decided to zip-line through the upper canopy of trees. Flying through the air is thrilling, but you'd be moving too fast to get good observations. Can you design a way to modify the zip line so that you're moving slowly enough to get a good view but not so slowly that you'll get stuck along the line?

▶ CHAPTER 8

MOTION

QUICK FACTS

Motion is happening everywhere, all the time. Motion can be upward, downward, forward, backward, sideways, or round and round. But motion can't just happen on its own. **FORCES ARE NEEDED TO GET SOMETHING MOVING**—and to keep it moving, stop it moving, or change direction. Without a force acting on an object, motion isn't possible.

The scientist ISAAC NEWTON (you've probably heard about him and his apple) stated THREE LAWS OF MOTION:

NEWTON'S FIRST LAW

AN OBJECT AT REST WILL STAY AT REST UNTIL A FORCE ACTS UPON IT.

Think about it: Your shoes are going to lie on your bedroom floor until you push them or pick them up. This law also applies to objects moving in a straight line. They'll keep right on moving until a force changes their direction.

NEWTON'S SECOND LAW

THE AMOUNT OF FORCE PLACED ON AN OBJECT—AND ALSO THE OBJECT'S MASS—AFFECTS ITS MOTION.

For example, if you push two identical tennis balls with different amounts of force, the ball you push with more force will move farther. If you push a bowling ball and a tennis ball with the same amount of force, the tennis ball will move farther because it has less mass.

NEWTON'S THIRD LAW

FOR EVERY ACTION THERE IS AN EQUAL AND OPPOSITE REACTION.

That's why your book doesn't fall through your desk to the floor—your desk is pushing up on your book with exactly the same amount of force that gravity is pulling down on your book.

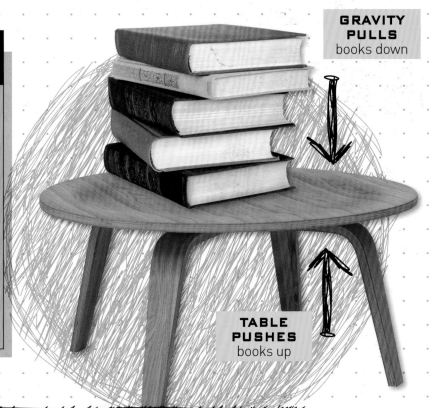

GRAVITY PULLS books down

TABLE PUSHES books up

LET'S GET ROLLING WITH MOTION.

DIFFICULTY

MINIMUM PEOPLE

BALLOON CAR

Newton's third law of motion says that forces always come in pairs: For every force acting on an object, there's another force of equal strength that's acting in the opposite direction. They're called **ACTION-REACTION PAIRS.** Most of the time, we don't notice the opposite force. For example, when you kick a ball, you exert force on it that sends it flying. But the ball exerts force back on your foot! Luckily for you, you're much heavier than the ball, so you don't go flying backward.

This law can be put to work in many useful ways. One of them is lifting a rocket off the launchpad. When the force of hot gas firing from the rocket pushes down against the ground, there is an equal force in the opposite direction that pushes up, causing the rocket to launch off the pad. Try it for yourself!

WHAT YOU'LL NEED

- Balloon

- Straight (non-bendy) paper or reusable drinking straw

- Rubber band

- Tape

- Small toy car

- A flat, smooth floor (carpeted floors will not work for this activity)

WHAT TO DO

1 **INSERT** one end of the straw into the balloon, then loop the rubber band around the mouth of the balloon until the straw is firmly secured in place.

2 **USE** the tape to secure the balloon to the top of the toy car. The straw should be pointing toward the back of the car.

3 **BLOW INTO THE STRAW** to fully inflate the balloon. When the balloon is fully inflated, cover the end of the straw so the air can't escape.

4 **REMOVE** your finger to release the straw, and off it goes!

THINK ABOUT IT

How could you use Newton's laws to make your race car even better? Make some adjustments, then challenge your friends to a race!

WHAT'S GOING ON?

Thanks to the straight line of the straw, the released air moves out from the balloon in a straight line. The opposite reaction pushing back, thrust, pushes the car forward in a straight line. If you raced a friend, who won? Why? There could be many factors at work: If your straw wasn't taped on straight, the air would have pushed out in a direction that wasn't exactly opposite to the direction the toy car's wheels are pointing. Whose car was heavier? Remember Newton's third law, which states that mass has an effect on motion.

DIFFICULTY

MINIMUM PEOPLE

GRAB AN ADULT!

STOMP ROCKET

Whether a rocket makes it to outer space or barely makes it off the launchpad depends on many factors. Most importantly, the rocket needs enough force to propel it out of Earth's atmosphere.

With air resistance, gravity, and other forces acting against the rocket's upward motion, rocket engineers need to calculate just how much force it will take to push the rocket hard enough to escape Earth's atmosphere. This is called the **ESCAPE VELOCITY.** It can be a tricky number to calculate—the force needs to be high enough to escape Earth but low enough to keep the rocket from getting damaged. Try it for yourself!

- Construction paper

- A PVC or metal pipe that is ½ inch (1 cm) wide and 12 to 24 inches (30 to 61 cm) long

- Clear tape

- Pencil

- Scissors

- Duct tape

- Markers or crayons

- An empty, clean, 2-liter flexible plastic bottle (like a soda or water bottle)

- Approximately 6 inches (15 cm) of flexible tubing, such as a vacuum hose or a bicycle inner tube

- A friend

WHAT TO DO

1   ROLL the paper around the pipe. Don't roll it too tightly. The rolled paper should be able to slide freely along the pipe without being too loose. Keep the paper tube closed with the clear tape, then slide the paper off the pipe. Use additional tape if needed to ensure the cylinder does not unravel. This will become the base for your rocket.

2   IN THE NEXT FEW STEPS, you'll create a nose cone for your rocket. Using the pencil, draw a semicircle on a piece of construction paper, using one of the shorter sides of the paper as the straight edge.

3   CUT the semicircle from the paper.

CONTINUE TO NEXT PAGE

WHAT TO DO (CONT'D)

4 ROLL the semicircle so it forms a cone with a pointed top. Continue to roll it tighter until it is approximately the width of the cylinder you made in step 1. Once the cone is the right size, tape the paper in place so it won't unroll.

5 USE scissors to trim the bottom off the cone so it's straight all around.

6 INSPECT the pointy end of the cone. If it's not sealed tight at the tip, seal it with a piece of tape to ensure no air can escape.

7 USING THE CLEAR TAPE, attach the cone to the cylinder you made in step 1. Ensure there is a tight seal. Now you have a rocket with a nose cone attached.

8 IF YOU WISH, add fins to the rocket to help stabilize the rocket's flight path. You can make these out of construction paper. Then set the rocket aside.

9 NOW IT'S TIME to make a launcher. Unscrew the cap from your bottle. Connect the bottle opening to the hose and secure it with duct tape. Make sure that there is a tight seal.

10 CONNECT the pipe to the open end of the hose using the duct tape. Ensure that there is a tight seal.

11 SLIP the rocket you designed onto the end of the pipe.

12 TAKE YOUR ROCKET and rocket launcher outside. Find a space large enough to launch your rocket safely.

13 HAVE A FRIEND POINT the rocket in the direction you would like it to launch, being careful to hold onto the pipe and not the rocket itself. Make sure the rocket is not pointed at another person. The rocket should be pointed into open space.

7

9

10

WHAT TO DO (CONT'D)

14 STOMP on the bottle to launch your rocket!

15 TO LAUNCH AGAIN, blow into the pipe to reinflate the bottle.

WHAT'S GOING ON?

When you stomp on the bottle, you force all of the air out of the bottle and through the tubing and the pipe. The force of air reaches the rocket and gives it the energy it needs to launch off the launchpad.

THINK ABOUT IT

How much force did you need to launch your rocket? What would happen if you stepped lightly on the bottle? What would happen if you jumped hard on it?

HOLD ON TIGHT!

HAVE YOU EVER SEEN FIRE-FIGHTERS USING A BIG FIRE HOSE TO SPRAY WATER? It takes a lot of strength to hold the hose in place. Usually, two or three firefighters are needed. This is because while the water is being pushed out of the hose with such a great force, an equal and opposite force is acting on the hose itself, almost like a rocket engine. The firefighters need to use their strength to offset the force against the hose.

DIFFICULTY

MINIMUM PEOPLE

STRAW ROCKET

To really play around with the idea of escape velocity, you'll need more control over the amount of force applied to your rocket. How much force will it take to launch a rocket as high as it will go? How much will it take to launch a rocket to a specified height? Build a straw rocket and try it for yourself!

WHAT YOU'LL NEED

- A sheet of paper

- Markers, crayons, or colored pencils

- Scissors

- A thin, bendy drinking straw

- A thicker drinking straw. The thin drinking straw should be able to slide into this straw.

- Tape

WHAT TO DO

1 ON THE PAPER, draw a picture of a rocket ship. Use the markers, crayons, or colored pencils to make the rocket ship colorful. Get creative!

2 CUT OUT the rocket ship using the scissors.

3 COMPLETELY SEAL one end of the thicker straw with tape. Tape the straw to the back of the rocket ship cutout, with the sealed-off end at the top of the rocket ship.

4 SLIP the thin straw into the thicker straw with the bendy part sticking out the bottom.

5 GO OUTSIDE or to a space with plenty of room. Blow into the end of the thin straw with a big puff of air. Liftoff!

WHAT'S GOING ON?

When you blow through the thin straw, the force of your air rushes up and hits the sealed-off top of the thicker straw. That pushes the thicker straw and rocket off into the air. The amount of force (air) you need to launch your rocket depends on how heavy your rocket is and its shape: Too much surface area will cause too much air resistance.

THINK ABOUT IT

What would happen if you made your rocket out of other kinds of paper or poster board? What would happen if you made the shape of your rocket narrower or wider? Try it and find out!

HOVER-CRAFT

DIFFICULTY

MINIMUM PEOPLE

GRAB AN ADULT!

Imagine rolling a ball across the floor. It doesn't roll forever, does it? Eventually it stops. Why? It stops because friction works against motion. When objects rub against each other, there is **FRICTION.** When the ball is rolled across the floor, the surface of the ball rubs against the surface of the floor.

Some surfaces create more friction than others. If you roll the ball across a gravel driveway it probably won't get as far as if you rolled that same ball across an ice patch. That's because the ice—a smooth surface—creates less friction than the gravel—a rough surface. Try it for yourself!

WHAT YOU'LL NEED

- Hot glue

- Pop-top "sports cap" from a water bottle or dish soap bottle

- An old CD or DVD that you no longer need

- A balloon

- A smooth table surface or hardwood floor

WHAT TO DO

1   ASK AN ADULT to use the hot glue to secure the sports cap to the CD so that it covers the hole in the center of the CD.

2   ONCE THE GLUE IS COMPLETELY DRY, lay the CD flat against a table. Ensure the sports cap is closed by pushing down on it.

3   COMPLETELY INFLATE the balloon and pinch the neck so air cannot escape. Twist the neck of the balloon several times to ensure no air escapes.

4   WHILE CONTINUING TO HOLD the balloon closed, carefully stretch the neck of the balloon around the closed sports cap so the cap is completely covered. This is your hovercraft.

5   LETTING GO OF THE BALLOON, give the hovercraft a little shove across the table and see how far it travels.

6   NOW PULL THE SPORTS CAP to its open position with the balloon still stretched over it. Give the hovercraft a little shove across the table. How does it travel?

WHAT'S GOING ON?

When the cap is closed, the CD moves against the table and experiences friction. This friction keeps the hovercraft from moving smoothly. When the cap is open, the balloon forces air out through the cap, creating a thin cushion of air between the CD and the table's surface. This cushion of air reduces the friction between the CD and the table, allowing the hovercraft to glide more smoothly and quickly.

💡 THINK ABOUT IT

Do you think your hovercraft would travel farther or more smoothly with a larger balloon? Why or why not? Experiment with your hovercraft on several different surfaces. Does the hovercraft work differently on carpet? On grass?

WARMING UP TO FRICTION

WHEN AN OBJECT MOVES AGAINST A SURFACE, IT SLOWS DOWN BECAUSE OF FRICTION. The object might lose speed, but the energy from its movement doesn't disappear. It just changes from moving energy to a different kind of energy: heat. Have you ever been outside in the cold and rubbed your hands together to try to get warm? Rubbing your hands together creates friction, and the friction generates heat. It's a great trick to keep in mind if you forget your mittens at home on a cold day!

Understanding motion can help in a lot of situations! Take a look at these scenarios, then grab your makerbox. Can you tinker up some ideas to get your solutions moving? Remember, there's no right answer!

SITUATION #1

You're an oceanographer studying samples from the ocean floor.

While you keep watch on the ship, your partner dives below. Quickly she realizes that she's left her waterproof notebook up on board. Can you build an instrument that can descend to the depths of the ocean and deliver the notebook without getting the paper wet, then launch itself back up to the surface?

SITUATION #2

You're a scientist studying glaciers in Iceland.

You decide to study the glaciers up close and there's no better way to observe them than to climb the glacial mountains for yourself. But the surface is slippery, even in your best hiking boots. What can you add to your hiking boots to improve traction so you can safely climb the ice?

SITUATION #3

It's been a good day backpacking a long stretch of the Appalachian Trail.

You covered many miles today, but your feet are starting to ache. You sit down for a rest and take off your hiking shoes to stretch your tired feet. You notice a blister on your big toe where the skin must've been rubbing up against your shoe. Can you think of something that might help minimize the friction to avoid additional pesky blisters?

SITUATION #4

After several days of steering your mokoro, or canoe, through the waters of the Okavango Delta, you come to a spot where the water has mostly dried up.

Your mokoro is full of supplies and would be too heavy to carry. Can you design a way to move your canoe across the drier spots to get back to where the water is deeper and flowing again?

AFTERWORD

ANYONE CAN BE A MAKER. IF YOU HAVE A PROBLEM, GATHER UP YOUR MAKING TOOLS AND GET TO WORK. DESIGN AND BUILD A SOLUTION! ALL IT TAKES IS A SPARK OF IMAGINATION—AND THE WILLINGNESS TO TRY, FAIL, AND TRY AGAIN.

As you've learned from this book, you don't need a lot of fancy gear and equipment to be a maker. All you need are some common materials from around the house to build some nifty contraptions—or at least models of solutions that can be manufactured on a larger scale. Reduce, reuse, and recycle—it's the maker way!

While craft sticks, paper towel tubes, and rubber bands can go a long way, many advanced makers rely on more cutting-edge tools and technologies to bring their maker ideas to life.

3D PRINTERS are popular in many community makerspaces. Unlike your average printer that creates an image on a sheet of paper, a 3D printer creates an object. You can print just about anything.

Imagine you lose a piece from one of your board games. That's pretty annoying! But with a 3D printer, you won't have to buy a replacement piece. You can just print it. What if you want to bring one of your superhero drawings to life? A 3D printer can create a perfect action figure.

Today, many organizations are starting to explore 3D printing to solve complicated problems. Engineers at NASA even built a rocket engine using a 3D printer. Some automobile companies are investigating 3D-printed parts for cars, and doctors are researching ways to 3D-print organs to help cure certain medical conditions.

ROBOTICS is another emerging technology for makers. Robotics is a field that often combines electronics, computers, and programming to build a machine. Some robots are simple and do nothing more than move in a straight line. Other, more high-tech, robots can execute complicated

tasks like working on an assembly line or performing medical procedures.

To get started making with robotics, you may want to look at purchasing a commercial kit that comes with the tools you need. Some kits contain a small circuit board that can control your inventions. It works by connecting to software running on a computer. The software uploads instructions to the circuit board, which controls your invention. Others provide a small inexpensive computer that allows you to program it with simple coding.

Whether you're making with recycled materials or complicated electronics, and whether your making takes the form of crafting or tinkering, you're putting your creativity to the test to solve a problem. So get going! You never know what amazing solutions will stem from creative playing. In fact, it may not be play at all!

MAKING IN THE FIELD

DID YOU ENJOY THE **SOLVE THIS! SCENARIOS IN THIS BOOK?**

Believe it or not, National Geographic Explorers (our intrepid scientists, researchers, conservationists, and photographers) face similar situations all the time while they're out in the field. What do you do when your camping stove breaks in the middle of a 10-day trek? Or when an interesting insect scuttles by in the middle of the desert? You've got to think fast, use what's around you, and get creative.

HERE ARE SOME REAL-LIFE SITUATIONS THAT EXPLORER SHAH SELBE ENCOUNTERED OUT IN THE FIELD.

Jacob Lewallen checks one of the water sensors in the Okavango Delta.

The Okavango Delta in Botswana is a very flat place, as many wetlands tend to be. I was installing a bunch of sensors in an area, and we needed them to be able to talk to each other—and to us—using radio waves. The higher in the air radio waves travel, the farther they can go. That can be hard to set up in a place that is mostly water and very flat, though. The solution we found ended up making use of some help from nature. Termites in this area build huge mounds of dirt as their homes. Some of these mounds can even grow big enough to support plants and trees on them! When I was deploying the sensors, I installed the radio on the highest termite mound I could find. This allowed us to talk to a bunch of sensors in the area, much more than would be possible if we just mounted it just above the water. We couldn't have made that project successful without our termite friends!

Shah repairs one of the early drones he used for ocean conservation.

While on expedition to a very remote part of California, I ended up crashing a drone on one of its first test flights. Normally that wouldn't be a problem—most drones have replaceable parts. For this expedition, though, it was different. This project used drones for ocean conservation in areas near the shore and along the coast. Because we had very special requirements for the drones, we had to build them all from scratch. That meant many of the parts were custom-made and we wouldn't be able to bring replacements. Because of the way my drone crash landed, I ended up breaking the mount for the camera. The camera was important because it was the only way we would be able to catch the poachers out at sea! So I had to quickly improvise to create a new mount. I used what I had around me: some cardboard, my shoelace, and some wire. It ended up working well for the rest of the expedition! Once I got back to the lab, though, we were luckily able to 3D-print a new part.

We were on expedition on a glacier in Banff National Park in Canada. I was building sensors that we deployed around the glacier that would monitor how fast the glacier was melting. The weather on glaciers can be quite dramatic and change pretty instantaneously. Fortunately, it was pretty nice for much of the sensor build. But, as we finished the solar panel installation, we realized that the connectors on the wire were not correct. So we had to fix it there, and just as we started the weather started to turn bad. The winds were some of the most intense I have experienced! The fix involved us soldering a new connector on the wire, and the winds made it too cold to get that to work. In order to make a protected place to fix the wire, we ended up taking a tarp (which we had used to protect some of the tools during the nights) and some wire to create a weather-protected work tent. Fixing the wire while protected from that cold wind was exactly what was needed to get the system running!

Shah starts up a sensor prototype on the Bow Glacier.

ALL PHOTOS WERE TAKEN BY MATTHEW RAKOLA, UNLESS OTHERWISE NOTED BELOW. ALL ILLUSTRATIONS BY SANJIDA RASHID.

YOU'LL FIGURE IT OUT!

Every day, all over the world, problems are being solved by engineers and creative people who can noodle their way through sticky situations to find solutions.

With this fun book, you'll learn how to put the principles of engineering to work in all kinds of wacky, real-life challenges—from soundproofing your bedroom to building your own outdoor play structure to removing hot pepper sauce from a swimming pool (ouch!).

CHECK OUT THE **SITUATION!**

NAT GEO EXPLORER
SOLUTIONS

Challenge #14: Remove Hot Pepper Sauce From the Swimming Pool

DIVIDE AND CONQUER

ERIKA
Deep-Sea Submersible Pilot

DESCRIBE YOUR SOLUTION.
Yikes! The first thing to do will be to keep the spill contained, *fast*! First I'd turn off the jets and pumps to keep water from mixing the sauce around. Next I'd make a containment boom by taping a pool noodle lengthwise along a towel. I'd dip the towel into the water on the outermost edge of the spill, curve the ends of the noodle toward the side of the pool, then stick the noodle to the edge of the pool with duct tape. I'd take the towel's bottom corners and slowly lift them up to the surface. The material is coated in sticky, wet taco sauce, but the water is (mostly) clean!

WHY DID YOU CHOOSE THESE SPECIFIC MATERIALS AND TOOLS?
I didn't have to leave home to clean up the mess! A towel, pool noodle, and duct tape are common items. Using readily available materials made it possible to build the containment barrier fast enough to contain the spill. Since the taco sauce is water-soluble, it spreads in water. Even though the oil in it separates and is fairly easy to scoop off the top, the vinegar and pepper ingredients would have been very difficult to filter if they had spread into the entire body of water. The noodle was vital to stopping that from happening. Another option was baking soda, which could be poured onto the spill to neutralize the acidic taco sauce. I also thought about trying to use a shop vac, which could filter water, but the volume of water was too great.

HOW COULD YOUR SOLUTION BE USED FOR A REAL-WORLD PROBLEM?
Containment booms are used in oil spills. When an oil drill in the ocean breaks and oil gushes into the water, the crew rapidly deploys an oilproof net to stop oil from leaking outside the immediate spill area.

SUPER SCOOPER

RYAN
Coral Reef Biologist

WHAT WAS YOUR FIRST IDEA? WAS IT YOUR BEST ONE?
My first idea was to remove the sauce from the water with something like a coffee filter inside of a strainer. I don't think it was my best plan. It would take quite a lot of time to siphon enough water to remove all of the sauce from the pool, and it might not be effective if the sauce was too thick or the filter got too wet. Instead, my solution would be to tape enough pool noodles together to span the width of the entire pool. The noodles could be pushed across the water to contain the spill in one area, making it easy to collect the sauce with a pool skimmer or bucket.

WHAT WERE YOUR CRITERIA FOR A SUCCESSFUL SOLUTION?
1) Enough sauce was removed to ensure the pool filter didn't become clogged.
2) The water didn't smell like sauce or sting the eyes more than usual.
3) The materials used were easily found near the pool.
4) Most of the pool's original water was retained.

QUICK THINKING

CINDY
Geologist

DESCRIBE YOUR SOLUTION.
Empty the air out of the beach ball and make a small hole on the side opposite the air nozzle. Put your mouth on the beach ball's air nozzle and aim the hole at the contaminated water. Inhale to create suction, then suck the hot sauce and contaminated water into the beach ball. Remove the ball from the pool and dump out the contaminated water. Repeat as needed.

WHAT WERE YOUR FIRST THOUGHTS WHEN YOU READ THE CHALLENGE?
At first I wasn't sure how to handle the problem, but I kept thinking about what materials were around the pool and how they could be most helpful for a quick and easy solution. I ran through my head what the scenario would look like, and kept rereading the question.

WHAT OTHER SOLUTIONS DID YOU CONSIDER?
I thought of grabbing a towel and trying to soak up the contaminated pool water. I knew this would only work if the hot sauce stayed in a small, concentrated area, not if it spread throughout the entire pool. It took me about 10 minutes of thinking before I came to my best solution!

More Solutions

122 / 123

NAT GEO ENGINEER
SOLUTIONS

Challenge #14: Remove Hot Pepper Sauce From the Swimming Pool

THE NAT GEO ENGINEERS REALLY DOVE INTO THIS ONE! TWO FAVORITE IDEAS BUBBLED TO THE TOP: ISOLATING THE SPILL TO SUCK IT OUT OF THE POOL AND MAKING A MAKESHIFT EXTRA-STRENGTH FILTER.

TOSS FLOAT RING OVER SPILL!

USE PILLOW STUFFING TO FILTER SAUCE

BRAD
My idea, well, you're in a swimming pool, so you're going to have floaty toys. If you have access to a floaty ring, throw that over the spill to contain it.

Another thing you could do is build a superstrong filter using charcoal. Take a five-gallon (19-L) bucket and poke a hole near the bottom of the bucket so the newly cleaned water will be able to drain back into the pool.

CHARCOAL

GET OUT OF THE POOL OR GET SOME GOGGLES! YOU DON'T WANT HOT SAUCE IN YOUR EYES. TRUST US!

USE CHARCOAL TO PURIFY WATER

MIKE

SLURP TACO SAUCE THROUGH STRAW

Then use a straw to suck up the part of the pepper sauce that's floating.*

Right. The only part of the pepper sauce people will see is the oily part floating on the surface. That's the part with the red pepper flakes. The rest of the sauce is colorless. It will sink into the pool water and disperse.

POKE HOLE IN BUCKET

REDIRECT WATER THROUGH EMERGENCY FILTER

Put a small pillow or cushion at the bottom of the bucket. That will prevent charcoal from getting into the pool. Now top the bucket with charcoal and put the bucket on the edge of the pool. Make a siphon by putting one end of some clean tubing in the pool and sucking on the other end to get the flow started. Direct the water through the filter and watch as hot sauce water flows into the bucket and clean water flows back into the pool.

*Be sure you don't let it get all the way to your mouth! The chemicals in the pool aren't good for drinking.

ERIC
The solution to pollution is dilution.

TOM
Couldn't we just blame a younger sibling?

124 / 125

For H, S, and N, my own special makers. —ES

The author and publisher wish to thank the book team: Shelby Lees, senior editor; Kathryn Williams, editorial assistant; Lori Epstein, photo director; Sanjida Rashid, art director and designer; Matthew Rakola, photographer; Grace Hill Smith and Robin Terry-Brown, text editors; Alix Inchausti, production editor; Anne LeongSon and Gus Tello, design production assistants; Julide Dengel for the generous use of her house; and the wonderfully creative volunteer Makers.

Since 1888, the National Geographic Society has funded more than 12,000 research, exploration, and preservation projects around the world. The Society receives funds from National Geographic Partners, LLC, funded in part by your purchase. A portion of the proceeds from this book supports this vital work. To learn more, visit natgeo.com/info.

For more information, visit nationalgeographic.com, call 1-800-647-5463, or write to the following address:

National Geographic Partners
1145 17th Street N.W.
Washington, D.C. 20036-4688 U.S.A.

Visit us online at nationalgeographic.com/books

For librarians and teachers: ngchildrensbooks.org

More for kids from National Geographic:
natgeokids.com

National Geographic Kids magazine inspires children to explore their world with fun yet educational articles on animals, science, nature, and more. Using fresh storytelling and amazing photography, *Nat Geo Kids* shows kids ages 6 to 14 the fascinating truth about the world—and why they should care.
kids.nationalgeographic.com/subscribe

For information about special discounts for bulk purchases, please contact National Geographic Books Special Sales: specialsales@natgeo.com

For rights or permissions inquiries, please contact National Geographic Books Subsidiary Rights: bookrights@natgeo.com

Designed by Sanjida Rashid

Library of Congress Cataloging-in-Publication Data

Names: Schwartz, Ella, 1974- author. | National Geographic Kids (Firm), publisher. | National Geographic Society (U.S.)
Title: Make this! / by Ella Schwartz.
Description: Washington, DC : National Geographic Kids, [2019] | Audience: Ages 8-12. | Audience: Grades 4 to 6.
Identifiers: LCCN 2018031314| ISBN 9781426333248 (pbk.) | ISBN 9781426333255 (hardcover)
Subjects: LCSH: Simple machines--Juvenile literature. | Tools--Juvenile literature. | Handicraft--Juvenile literature.
Classification: LCC TJ147 .S437 2019 | DDC 621.8/11--dc23
LC record available at https://lccn.loc.gov/2018031314

Printed in China
18/RRDS/1